Sola Scriptura
and Sectarianism

Sola Scriptura and Sectarianism

The Rise of the Rogerenes in Colonial New London, 1664 – 1721

by
Susan Lim, Ph.D.

Cheshire, CT

© 2019 Susan Lim

No part of this book may be reproduced or utilized in any form or by any means, including photocopying, recording, or by any information storage and retrieval system, without express permission in writing from the publisher.

Published by The Connecticut Press
All inquiries should be addressed to:
The Connecticut Press
36 Wildlife Court
Cheshire, CT 06410
www.connecticutpress.com

First Edition

Cataloguing-in-Publication Data

Lim, Susan, author
    Sola Scriptura and Sectarianism: The Rise of the Rogerenes in Colonial New London, 1664 – 1721, 163 pp. Includes annotations, bibliography, and index
    ISBN 978-0-9977907-4-0 (softcover)
    Library of Congress Control Number: 2019951321

1. History–America–Connecticut–New London–Colonial History | 2. Biography–John Rogers (1648 – 1721) | Religion–Rogerenes | 3. Sectarianism | 4. Congregationalists | 5. Dissidents

Designed and Printed in the United States of America

Table of Contents

Acknowledgments ix

Introduction... xi

Chapter 1.. 1
A New Religion

Chapter 2 19
The Sabbath

Chapter 3 35
Religious License

Chapter 4 53
Doctrines of Man and the Role of the Spirit

Chapter 5 73
Methods and Matters of Dissent

Chapter 6 91
Family Matters

Conclusion 109

Notes on Sources... 123

Bibliography 135

Index 157

Acknowledgements

Like most books, this one also has a history. And many talented and kind people helped bring this manuscript to publication. Although the dissertation form of this work was substantially different, the premise of the book was conceived during my graduate-school years at UCLA. The Rogerenes became the primary focus of this study under the expert guidance of Joyce Appleby, who guided this research process, chaired my committee, and graciously took me under her wings as her very last student prior to retirement. Her mentorship, then subsequent friendship, have been blessings in my life. I miss her terribly and only wish that she were still on this earth to see this work in published form. I am certain that she is cheering me on from heaven.

Many friends and family members encouraged me in countless ways: Soo Jin Lee, Grace Kim, and, of course, Jessie Chung are the foremost in my mind. Each of their lives reflect such beauty and strength that inspire me in every facet of my life. Thank you for making this world a better place. And to my parents, parents-in-law, and siblings, Jennifer Kim and Henry Kim, thank you for your prayers that sustained me during this long and arduous process of writing.

I had the good fortune of meeting Robert Middlekauff while I was a visiting scholar at Berkeley. Since, he has been an invaluable mentor who has offered priceless words of wisdom and encouragement. Under his guidance, I was able to publish my very first peer-reviewed journal article, and he has generously read drafts of this entire manuscript, providing insightful edits and feedback. In all things academic and scholarly, Bob's reputation speaks for itself. Perhaps people who only know him by these impressive accomplishments might not be aware of his generosity and kindness. Bob perfectly demonstrates what brilliance and humility look like in tandem. Thank you, Bob, from the bottom of my heart.

Dearest to my heart and the biggest thank you goes to my family. Josephine and JD are the best kids that a mom could ever wish for. They studied, read, drew, and played video games (a little) alongside me as I wrote and then rewrote countless drafts of this manuscript. They surprised and encouraged me by bringing me snacks and doing unasked chores around the house so that I could write a little more. They found productive things to do when I took naps when I couldn't write anymore for the day. I love you both more than words can express. And, this book is dedicated to my husband and hero, Brian Lim. You are a prince among men. You have taught me what love looks like in the day-to-day. Your love has been the fuel for my soul. Every place that you tread is more hopeful, beautiful, and love-filled because of you. I love you and thank God daily for the gift of you.

SL
November 2019

Introduction

John Rogers has never been accused of orthodoxy, but that is the charge of this book. His unconventional antics and incendiary statements have earned Rogers a place amongst the radical sectarians in the colonies, but his writings suggest that a new portrayal is in order. Rogers dreamt along with the Puritans of a city on a hill where God's people lived by Scripture alone. Over and over again Rogers claimed to provide nothing but "Scripture Proofs" and "Scripture Reasons" to substantiate his views.[1] Though Rogers's version of a holy city differed dramatically from that of the Congregationalists', a careful culling of Rogers's treatises unearths surprising and often overlooked aspects of Rogers's staunch belief in Sola Scriptura. Rogers's own words prove that he was no antinomian.

The second of the two-fold aim of this study is to provide the first book-length research exclusively dedicated to Rogers and his followers, the Rogerenes. John Rogers holds a unique position in religious history as the founder of the first indigenous sect in the colonies.[2] Although the Rogerenes were superseded by sectarians such as the Hutchinsonians and Gortonists, they were the first religious dissenters led by a native-born colonist whose ideals were shaped by life in the New World. Unlike the sectarian leaders who preceded him, Rogers was born and bred in New London and did not have old world organizational ties to propel his ministry in the colonies. All of this indicates that a study of the Rogerenes is long overdue. With a rich legacy bequeathed by a print-loving people, the Rogerenes left many sources yet to be thoroughly dissected. There are forty-four identified titles authored by Rogerenes, with John Rogers as the most published writer. These tracts and treatises reveal the topsy-turvy spiritual terrain of Puritan New England and a man bent on anchoring himself in the Scriptures.

---

[1] John Rogers, A*n Answer to a Book Intituled, The Lords Day Proved to be the Christian Sabbath &c. By B. Wadsworth, A.M. Pastor of a Church in Boston. And also, An Answer to a Pamphlet, Intituled Thesis concerning the Sabbath. As Also, Some Part of what hath passed through the General Courts in Connecticut Colony, relating to the Sabbath. As Also, Some Court Sentences in that Colony, by John Rogers* (Boston: n.p., 1721), 13.

[2] John L. Brooke, *The Refiner's Fire: The Make of Mormon Cosmology, 1644-1844* (Cambridge: Cambridge University Press, 1994), 48; Carla Pestana, *Liberty of Conscience and the Growth of Religious Diversity in Early America, 1636-1786* (Providence: John Carter Brown Library, 1986), 56-7.

By 1677 when Rogers formed the Rogerenes, the Puritans were crying declension. Apparently, the spiritual decline had been quick and steep. Shortly after John Winthrop and his fellow Puritans stepped of the decks of the *Arabella* in 1630, New Englanders were at odds with one another. Dissenters splintered off in an array of trajectories, and people like Anne Hutchinson and Roger Williams found themselves banished from the Congregational fold. In the following decades, the Half-Way Covenant was issued indicating that second-generation Puritans could not reach the standards of their fathers. The fear of declension seemed an unfortunate reality for these first-generation immigrants.

In the decade following this halfway compromise, a new dissenting group appeared in the seaport town of New London. There the trading market bustled with vigor and enterprise, and ambitious men came from distant shores to make their fortune. From time to time, commercial aspirations were coupled with religious ones, and Sabbatarians, Quakers, Anabaptists, and other dissenters infiltrated the market to make money and, perhaps, converts. These sectarian traders had a profound impact on John Rogers, who was a merchant himself.

Though Rogers never traveled across the Atlantic Ocean, he spent countless hours with men who had. Sectarians from England and Ireland often met with Rogers for months at a time, and Quakers and Sabbatarians (known as Seventh-Day Baptists) from the Old World influenced Rogers's thoughts on doctrine and society. These traders, and others from the Atlantic world, aided Rogers's exit from the Congregational fold in 1674.[3] The following three years were ones of intense spiritual examination, and Rogers spent many hours studying the Scriptures. In 1677, he came to the conclusion that to stay true to the Bible meant establishing his own faith altogether. From this point until his death in 1721, Rogers seized every opportunity, whether in print or in person, to teach the Scriptures without distortion. Disagreements, of course, arose over whose interpretation of Scripture was true; but that the Scriptures should be preeminent in colonial New London was never questioned by Rogers or the Congregationalist leaders.

The nearly five-decade struggle between the Rogerenes and the

---

[3] Susan Lim, "The Rise of the Rogerenes in Colonial New London," *Connecticut History* 47, no. 2 (2008): 237-251.

Standing Order has left a lasting portrayal of John Rogers as a fanatical sectarian leader. Little has been written about Rogers beyond his boisterous demonstrations, and he and his followers are generally characterized as the radical dissenters whom the Puritans loved to hate. A more accurate depiction of the Puritan-Rogerene relationship is in order through in-depth examinations of Rogers's writings. John Rogers's publications reveal that he was more of an intellectual than a rioter. In the thickest of battles, Rogers picked up the pen rather than the sword and used his words to challenge the Congregational order. Rogers covered a broad range of issues in his writings, which could be categorized loosely as commentaries on religious and political affairs in New London. Rogers's core belief in the Scriptures was woven into these two spheres of colonial life, and his writings clearly proposed that both church and state powers submit to biblical precepts.

Most of Rogers's writings expressed his dissatisfaction with the Puritans who dominated Connecticut civil and religious affairs. Rogers believed that the Congregationalists in charge of New London, and Connecticut, were erroneously interpreting the Holy texts. Rogers's critics, both clerics and laymen, responded forcibly in pamphlets, sermons, and legal discourses.[4] Rogers's contemporaries dissected his deeds and ideas not only in public documents, but also in private writings such as letters and diary entries. These written affronts against the Rogerenes are also a part of the largely unmined primary sources for those studying the sect. Mixing these voices with Rogers's own will recreate a fuller dialogue of these eventful conversations.

Though the Rogerenes extensively used print to defend themselves, their opponents were far more prolific and widely read. Rogerene writers were certainly no match for Gurdon Saltonstall, James Noyes, John Woodward, and other such ecclesiastical and community leaders. Hence, accounts of Rogerene misgivings were often believed over counter-testimonies written by these sectarians. Many Congregationalists viewed Rogerenes as tares among the wheat and as sinners tempting God's wrath to be unleashed upon New London. Treatises written by Rogerenes were derided as emotional tirades replete with trumped-up

---

[4] Francis Manwaring Caulkins, *History of New London, Connecticut: From the First Survey of the Coast in 1612, to 1860* (New London: H.D. Utley, 1895), 203-4.

tales that exaggerated their persecutions and hardships as unjust.

Credibility of authorship is also a problem when appraising secondary literature. Most secondary literature solely about the Rogerenes has been written by Rogerene descendants in defense of their forefathers' beliefs or as genealogical works. Often, these writings pointedly come to the defense of their ancestors and are crafted with a personal agenda in mind. "A Vindication," the first part of the major secondary work on the Rogerenes, aptly describes these descendants' objectives.[5] Desiring to vindicate the Rogerene reputation, some authors have sanitized controversies within the Rogerene camp in order to create a harmonious past. For example, John Bolles insists that family relations remained friendly even after Jonathan Rogers denounced the Rogerene faith as heretical and continued to attend the Sabbatarian Church in Newport. Whether Jonathan remained on speaking terms with his family members and other Rogerenes until his death in 1697 is uncertain, but the friction that tainted their interaction is clear. Jonathan's refusal to admit to Sabbath-breaking before court authorities and his blatant contempt for faith-healing resulted in his expulsion from the Rogerenes. These were certainly unhappy times, although Bolles suggests otherwise.[6]

Rogerene accounts are also mentioned in New England histories, and notable historians have incorporated Rogerene history in their assessments of colonial American religion.[7] These inclusions have provided

---

[5] John R. Bolles and Anna B. Williams, *The Rogerenes: Some Hitherto Unpublished Annals Belonging to the Colonial History of Connecticut* (Boston: Stanhope Press, 1904).

[6] Ibid., 153, 159.

[7] Examples of Rogerenes mentioned in New England religious history: Patricia U. Bonomi, *Under the Cope of Heaven: Religion, Society, and Politics in Colonial America* (New York: Oxford University Press, 1986); Richard L. Bushman, *From Puritan to Yankee: Character and the Social Order in Connecticut, 1690-1765* (Cambridge: Harvard University Press, 1967); William G. McLoughlin, *New England Dissent, 1630-1833: The Baptists and the Separation of Church and State* (Cambridge: Harvard University Press, 1971); Carla Pestana, *Quakers and Baptists in Colonial Massachusetts* (New York: Cambridge University Press, 1991); Carla Pestana, *Protestant Empire: Religion and the Making of the British Atlantic World* (Philadelphia: University of Pennsylvania Press, 2009); Val D. Rust, *Radical Origins: Early Mormon Converts and Their Colonial Ancestors* (Chicago: University of Illinois Press, 2004). Also, the history of New London should be considered in the following studies: Edward E. Atwater, *History of the Colony of New Haven to Its Absorption in Connecticut* (Meriden: Journal Publishing, 1902); Charles McLean Andrews, *Connecticut's Place in Colonial History* (New Haven: Yale University Press, 1923); Lewis G. Knapp, *In Pursuit of Paradise: History of the Town of Stratford, Connecticut* (West Kennewbunk: Phoenix, 1923); Charles Edward Perry, ed., *Founders and Leaders of Connecticut, 1633-1783* (Boston: Heath, 1934); Louis B. Mason, *The Life and Times of Major John Mason of Connecticut, 1600-1672* (New York: G.P. Putnam's Sons, 1935); Gilman C. Gates, *Saybrook at the Mouth of Connecticut: The First One Hundred Years* (Orange: Wilson H. Lee, 1935); Rollin G. Osterweis, *Three Centuries of New Haven, 1638-1938* (New Haven: Yale University Press, 1953);

a more thorough overview of the New England theological landscape. The widening breadth, however, has not always been commensurate with depth since these Rogerene narratives serve as a backdrop to other interests. Mostly these studies offer standard commentary including familiar discussions of variant beliefs, disruptive demonstrations, and legal ramifications.

Several historians whose works have centered on Connecticut have been especially mindful of discussing the Rogerenes in their study of the past. Whether writing for Connecticut newspapers or for a larger audience, however, these historians have largely provided more commentary than analysis.[8] Although Connecticut historians have succeeded better at mining primary sources and etching in the details than have religious historians, their Rogerene accounts are not contextualized in a broader study of religious movements, nor do they explain why their findings are significant for the understanding of sectarians. The same is true for the works of Ellen Starr Brinton, one of the few historians of non-Rogerene descent to dedicate her work exclusively to this sect. She has written an eighteen-page article on Rogerene history and a twenty-two-page article listing books by and about the Rogerenes. Both works are helpful in amassing Rogerene data but lack analysis or in-depth examination of these findings.[9]

Only a few scholarly works dedicated solely to the Rogerenes exist, and two of these are doctoral dissertations. Grosskopf's important work on the Rogerenes reveal the intersection of religious dissent, colonial policies, and family history; and one of my articles on the Rogerenes investigates their rise in the midst of transatlantic exchanges. My other article is, in a sense, a precursor to this work as it hones in on the Rogerenes' adept usage of print as a method of dissent. None of these works, however, has resulted in a published monograph on this

---

W. Storrs Lee, *The Yankees of Connecticut* (New York: Henry Hold and Company, 1957); John Waters, "Family, Inheritance, and Migration in Colonial New England: The Evidence from Guilford, Connecticut," *William and Mary Quarterly*, XXXIX (1982), 64–86; Francis J. Degnan, *A New Look at Old New Haven (New Haven: Yale-New Haven Teachers Institute, 1992)..*

[8] Some Rogerene articles are intended for local audiences, such as Julie Q. Ladwig's "Few Traces Remain of Ledyard's Early Dissenters," in *Compass Comment* 2, 20.38 (Sept. 18, 1975), 4. This short article is available at the Groton Public Library, Mystic, Connecticut. Caulkins, *History of New London*; David M. Roth, *Connecticut: A Bicentennial History* (New York: Norton, 1979).

[9] Ellen Starr Brinton, "The Rogerenes," *New England Quarterly* 16, no. 1 (1943): 2-19, and Ellen Starr Brinton, *Books by and about the Rogerenes* (New York: The New York Public Library Bulletin, 1945).

unique religious group. The time has now come for such a contribution.[10]

Tilling new ground requires special sequencing. As such, the chapters of this book are arranged so that they address the second aim first. That is, I believe the right ordering of this undertaking would start with a proper introduction of the Rogerenes in both their genesis and development. Chapter 1 sets the New London stage in the latter third of the seventeenth century. In particular, the void in political and ecclesiastical leadership allowed for new ideas to germinate in colonial minds, and John Rogers adeptly filled that vacancy.

Rogers was the son of the wealthy and well-established James Rogers and leveraged his monetary and social advantages to further his sectarian interests. John Rogers's familial history in trading with European merchants became an important factor when in 1677 he founded his own sect, the Rogerenes. The first chapter also outlines key Rogerene beliefs. From the beginning, Rogers made it exceptionally clear that he and his followers believed in Scriptural mandates only. Ironically, Rogers claimed that his dissent stemmed *from* following the Bible and not as a result of his deviance from it.

The remaining chapters return to the first aim of this book. In turn, they examine Rogers's use of Scripture regarding the major theological debates of his time: the role of the Holy Spirit, the parameters of church and state, and the guidelines of proper worship and Sabbath keeping. Though it is hard for contemporary readers to imagine, these topics rivaled in intensity our current debates on subjects such as Black Lives Matter, DACA (Deferred Action for Childhood Arrivals), and funding for Planned Parenthood. Inherent in all of these dialogues, both present and past, is the question of power. Colonists spilled much ink and blood in defending their ideals and positions of power. Those who usurped and misused power in the name of God roiled Rogers the most. He struck back with a careful exposition of

---

[10] Denise [Jan] Schenk Grosskopf, "The Limits of Religious Dissent in Seventeenth-Century Connecticut: The Rogerene Heresy," (Ph.D. diss., University of Connecticut, 1999); Jan Schenk Grosskopf, "Family, Religion, and Disorder: The Rogerenes of New London, 1676-1726," *Connecticut History* 40 (Fall 2001): 203-24. Susan C. Kim [maiden name], "Mr. Rogers's Neighborhood: Religious Dissent in New London, 1674-1721," (Ph.D. diss., University of California, Los Angeles, 2006). Susan Lim, "The Rise of the Rogerenes in Colonial New London," *Connecticut History* 47 (Fall 2008): 237-51. Susan Lim, "Evangelization in Print: The Writings of the Rogerenes of New London, 1677-1721," *Connecticut History* 51, no. 2 (Fall 2012): 234-50.

Scripture to justify rightful power and nullify the counterfeit kinds.

Chapters two through five also reveal the person of John Rogers. From prominence to prison, Rogers's life had frequent ups and downs that matched the unsteady spiritual domain of New London. Through each hardship and victory, Rogers held fast to the Scriptures to explain how his earthly circumstances held eternal significance. His theological expositions frequently interconnected with his personal experiences, and his first marriage, in particular, played a pivotal role in forming his doctrinal views. When his first wife, Elizabeth Griswold Rogers, filed for divorce in 1675, she set a precedence in colonial American history by winning custody of their two children. Further, this divorce set Rogers on a path of no return that led him from the staunchest of conservatism to the extremes of religious dissent.

In all these matters, both personal and doctrinal, Rogers's adherence to the Scriptures is an about-face from the current historical narratives about this rogue dissenter. What sets Rogers apart is not his strident demonstrations but his insistence on keeping true to biblical precepts. Of course, anyone can wield bits and pieces of any sacred text and coopt the central message for something entirely unrecognizable, but Rogers's message does not. His aim of understanding the breadth and depth of Scripture comes through in his exposition of both the Old and New Testaments in their historical and interpretive contexts. Though some, or many, may disagree with Rogers's tenets, no one, after reading his words, may call him ignorant of the Scriptures.

Chapter 1

A New Religion

New London

Most of John Rogers's life was largely lived in New London, a town considered to be the laxest and freest in terms of religious toleration in all of Connecticut. Perhaps this stemmed from its closeness to Rhode Island and the influences from the "rogues" who resided there. A more significant reason for religious leniency in New London was because it was a port town, where disparate ideas ebbed and flowed as merchants and travelers passed through. The Congregational government controlled which items could be taxed, which goods could be consumed, and which books could be read; and persecution and stringent governance were a part of life, as was the case in any other colonial New England town. Sectarians, however, undoubtedly noticed religious tolerance in New London as they flocked to this port city in hopes of worshiping more freely than most New England towns permitted.

New London was a town with many commercial opportunities, but also a place with internal problems. A lack of leadership was painfully apparent in the 1660s and 1670s when John Winthrop, Jr. left New London in 1675 to serve as the governor of Connecticut. New Londoners looked to his sons, Fitz-John and Wait Still, to provide the leadership vacated by the elder Winthrop, but these inhabitants were sorely disappointed. Fitz-John Winthrop refused to serve the colony and exacerbated the weak leadership when he cohabited with a common-law wife, Elizabeth Tongue, with whom he fathered an illegitimate daughter in 1670. When New London formally constituted the church in 1670, an official church-membership list was penned. Only official church members could vote in town meetings and have a say in religious affairs, and Fitz-John Winthrop was not listed as a member. Wait Winthrop removed himself entirely from New London affairs and settled in Boston in 1670.

A lack of leadership coincided with a rapid increase in population. In New London there were fewer than fifty adult males in 1651, but that figure had more than doubled by 1660.[1] The rise in population, coupled with a weak leadership, meant that the Congregationalists in New London were not well situated to deal with the surge in variant religious ideals. Three-fourths of the New London settlers who arrived before 1660 were from Northwest England, an area known for its dissenting traditions.[2] An overall increase in sectarian presence was felt by 1700.

The New London population growth was the result of a general population growth in Connecticut. In 1656 there were approximately 800 male inhabitants in the colony, but that number expanded to 9,000 by 1665, 20,000 by 1689, and 50,000 by 1730. Much of the population boom could be attributed to migration, natural increase, and the incorporation of New Haven Colony into Connecticut. With the rising number of inhabitants came the settling of more sectarians in New London and other Connecticut cities.[3] For example, Anglicans in Old England founded the Society for the Propagation of the Gospel in Foreign Parts (S.P.G.) as a missions organization in 1702, and they hoped to establish a sizeable number of Anglican churches in the colonies. Within decades Anglicans settled in Connecticut, with Stratford being the most occupied with fifty Episcopal families by 1727. New London had approximately one-hundred Anglicans by the end of 1730, and there were nearly seven-hundred Episcopal families in the entire colony of Connecticut by 1736.[4] The S.P.G. could not keep up with the influx of Anglicans, depriving many of a church of their own.

The entry of religious dissenters into Connecticut[5] and the

---

[1] Maria Louise Greene, *The Development of Religious Liberty in Connecticut* (Boston: Houghton, Mifflin, and Company, 1905), 173-74.

[2] Cedric B. Cowing, T*he Saving Remnant, Religion and the Settling of New England* (Urbana: University of Illinois Press, 1995), 24.

[3] Greene, *The Development of Religious Liberty*, 173-74.

[4] Anglicans comprised approximately one-seventh of the population in Stratford by 1727, which means that Anglicans composed fewer than one-seventh of the population for all the other colonies in Connecticut. E. Edwards Beardsley, *The History of the Episcopal Church in Connecticut from the Settlement of the Colony to the Death of Bishop Seabury* (New York: Hurd and Houghton, 1865), 60, 86-87, 105. Also helpful is Origen Storrs Seymour, *The Beginnings of the Episcopal Church in Connecticut* (New Haven: Yale University Press, 1934).

[5] Some dissenters chose to reside in nearby colonies, but still made their presence felt in Connecticut. For example, the Quakers made trips into New London and other New England cities to proselytize but permanent settlement was often chosen among their established cohorts in Penn's colony or Rhode Island.

growth of the colony in general brought its population to around 30,000 by 1701.[6] Perhaps as a measure of protection against sectarians and a means to control their increase, Congregationalists responded with the Saybrook Platform in 1708. This act, supported by Governor Gurdon Saltonstall, moved Congregationalists toward more of a Presbyterian structure and strengthened their uniformity. Church leaders still held that local towns were largely free to do as they chose, but the Saybrook Platform enforced the notion of corporate discipline and obeisance to a consociation.[7]

The rise of sectarian presence was especially troublesome to New London authorities since they lacked both religious and political leadership. Like many New England towns, New London had difficulties retaining a minister, and this inability took a toll on the inhabitants' spiritual development. Richard Blinman arrived from Gloucester in 1650 to serve as New London's first Congregational minister. Under his guidance, the first meetinghouse was built in 1655 but he left in 1658. His vacancy was not filled for two years, and between 1659 and 1660, visiting ministers or laymen took the Sunday pulpit. On certain occasions, Sunday worship was canceled altogether.[8]

Gershom Bulkley served as the town's minister between 1661 and 1666, but his short tenure caused more disruption to the religious stability of the local residents. His first year was spent in negotiations regarding matters of salary and duties, and the last year was filled with strife between Bulkley and the church members. Simon Bradstreet eventually replaced Bulkley in 1667 and served until his death in 1683. Though Bradstreet's occupancy provided a measure of healing, New London Congregationalists could not find a replacement for nearly eight years after his death. Gurdon Saltonstall arrived in New London in 1689 but did not officially serve as the pastor of the First Congregational Church until 1691. These were eight long years for New Londoners to be without an official pastor.

---

[6] Mary L. and William F. Swindler, eds., *Chronology and Documentary Handbook of the State of Connecticut* (Dobbs Ferry: Oceana Publications, Inc., 1973).
[7] Richard S. Dunn, *Puritans and Yankees: The Winthrop Dynasty of New England, 1630-1717* (New York: The Norton Library, 1971), 354-355; Richard L. Bushman, *From Puritan to Yankee: Character and the Social Order in Connecticut, 1690-1765* (Massachusetts: Harvard University Press, 1967), 150-54.
[8] Leroy S. Blake, *The Early History of the First Church of Christ in New London, Connecticut* (New London: Press of the Day Publishing Company, 1897), 69, 92-93.

Saltonstall finally brought order to the fluctuating religious milieu of New London during his service as pastor from 1691 through 1707. Later, in 1708 Saltonstall was elected governor of Connecticut, the first Congregational minister to hold a high colonial post, and he held the governorship until his death in 1724. Saltonstall did much to bring order and stability to New London religious and political affairs. Still, Congregational teaching and order had been compromised due to the vacancies and turmoil in religious leadership, and the rise of the Rogerenes is a telling example of such instability. The timing is no coincidence since the Rogerenes took hold in the 1680s, the very decade that New London struggled the most without a pastor.

The Birth of the Rogerenes

Connecticut has often been dubbed as the "land of steady habits" due to its moral rigidity, but New London proved to be an area of exception. This port city with unsteady religious leadership proved to be the perfect habitat where the Rogerenes could thrive. The vacancy in spiritual leadership opened the way to a powerful New London resident, John Rogers, founder and leader of the Rogerenes. He was the third son of James and Elizabeth Rogers, who were members of the First Congregational Church of Milford. The Rogers family moved from Milford to New London sometime between 1656 and 1660, and all records indicate that they transferred their allegiance and dedication to the First Congregational Church of New London upon their change of residence.[9]

Growing up in a home steeped in Puritan ideals afforded John Rogers and his siblings a strong Calvinist foundation. The Rogers children, Samuel, Joseph, John, Bathsheba, James, Jr., Jonathan, and Elizabeth, all received a traditional Congregational upbringing, with no hint of deviance, religious or otherwise.[10] John Rogers was a dutiful son,

[9] Elizabeth Rowland Rogers became a member in 1645 and James Rogers became a member in 1652. Frances Manwaring Caulkins, *History of New London, Connecticut: From the First Survey of the Coast in 1612 to 1860* (New London: H.D. Utley, 1895), 201.

[10] Their dates of birth, in chronological order, are as follows: Samuel, 1640; Joseph, 1646; John, 1648; Bathsheba, 1650; James, unrecorded; Jonathan, December 31, 1655; Elizabeth, 1658. Ellen Starr Brinton notes that John Rogers was the youngest son, but this statement does not match up with the existing birth records or certain life events of John Rogers. For example, John Rogers married Elizabeth Griswold in 1670. Had he been born after Jonathan in 1655, he would have been no more than a fourteen-year-old groom. Ellen Starr Brinton, "The Rogerenes," *New England Quarterly* 16 (1943): 5; Caulkins, *History of New London*, 201.

a contributing member of society, and a respectable leader of his own family after his marriage to Elizabeth Griswold on October 17, 1670. A year after his wedding, John Rogers became a father when Elizabeth was born on November 8, 1671; and three years later John, Jr. was born on March 20, 1674.[11]

The year of John Jr.'s birth is an important one because it coincided with Rogers's decision to leave his Congregational beliefs behind. Sabbatarians from Newport persuaded Rogers to reassess his theological beliefs and compare them with their own. Initially Rogers's interactions with these Sabbatarians served merely commercial purposes, since both parties were traders of merchandise.[12] As their relationship progressed from commercial to personal, Rogers found himself keenly drawn to these dissenters and their religious ideals.

The Newport Sabbatarian Church derived its theology from the Bell Lane Sabbatarian Church in England and organized in 1671 as an offshoot from the First Baptist Church in Newport. Like most denominations of Baptist persuasion, the Newport Sabbatarians baptized adults only by full immersion. And, as their name suggests, they observed their weekly Sabbath on Saturday, rather than Sunday. Sabbatarians subscribed to Calvinist ideals of predestination and also observed the Ten Commandments. Besides these doctrines, there was little overlap with Congregational beliefs. From denouncing the Trinity to opposing church taxes, the Sabbatarians stood at odds from the Congregationalist doctrines that John Rogers found familiar.

Rogers accepted the challenge to reassess his Congregational beliefs and soon found himself in a religious crisis. While dutifully studying Sabbatarian doctrines, Rogers felt a "deep conviction" from the "memory of a certain youthful error" that "weigh[ed] heavily upon his conscience." After much soul searching, Rogers experienced a "sudden and powerful conviction of sin" followed by freedom from a lifetime of shame and self-condemnation stemming from this indiscretion.[13] There have been

---
[11] Caulkins, *History of New London*, 203.
[12] For full details on how trade affected the creation of the Rogerenes, see Susan Lim, "The Rise of the Rogerenes in Colonial New London," *Connecticut History* 47, no. 2 (2008): 237-48.
[13] John Rogers, Jr., *An Answer to a Book lately put forth by Peter Pratt, Entituled, The Prey taken from the Strong. Wherein by Mocks and Scoffs, together with a great number of positive Falshoods, the Author hath greatly abused John Rogers, late of New-London, deceased, since his Death* (New York: n.p., 1726), 36, 42; Benjamin Trumbull, *A Complete History of Connecticut, Civil and Ecclesiastical, From the Emigration*

unsubstantiated allegations that this "youthful error" was either Rogers's purported dabbling in bestiality or that he had illegitimately fathered a child with a slave woman. Both charges have never been proven in court or otherwise. Though his transgression was never named specifically, in 1674, Rogers proclaimed that God had finally removed "the Guilt of my Sins from my Conscience" by sending "the Spirit of his Son into my heart." He had experienced a new birth, or what he defined as "the work of regeneration."[14]

After this powerful conversion experience, Rogers left the Congregational church and started sharing his new Sabbatarian beliefs with those nearest to him. He explained to his family that Sabbatarianism provided a truer, more authentic path to God since it was through this doctrine that he gained a regenerated life. The particular doctrine that Rogers found especially compelling centered around the Sabbath. The Sabbatarians adhered to a Saturday rest and denounced the concept and constrictions of the Congregational Sabbath. The Congregational rules and regimen mirrored that of the Pharisees, and liberty from such constraints exemplified the freedom that Rogers felt from his guilty conscience. It is no surprise that Rogers would later pen many pages defending his concept of the Sabbath.

Most of his immediate family members found Rogers's arguments for the Sabbatarian doctrine compelling. Rogers and his brother, James, Jr., immediately opted for baptism, and John Crandall, a former elder at the Baptist Church in Westerly, had the honor of performing this rite in 1674. Within the next three years, most of the Rogers family was baptized into the Sabbatarian fold. To further cement their ties, on March of 1678, Jonathan Rogers married Naomi Burdick, daughter of one of the Sabbatarian elders at Newport.[15]

Choosing to follow the Sabbatarian way was costly, and the Rogers family immediately felt the pinch. John Rogers, who became a shoemaker in 1675, chose to labor on Sundays since he now chose Sat-

---

of its First Planters, from England, in the Year 1630, to the Year 1764; and to the Close of the Indian Wars (New London: H.D. Utley, 1898), II:20; Private Controversies, Connecticut Archives, Series 2, VI: 132d.

[14] John R. Bolles and Anna B. Williams, *The Rogerenes: Some Hitherto Unpublished Annals Belonging to the Colonial History of Connecticut* (Boston: Stanhope Press, 1904), 127; John Rogers, *An Epistle to the Churches of Christ call'd Quakers; And another epistle to the Seventh Day Baptists, with several Theological Essays* (New York: William Bradford, 1705), vi-vii.

[15] Blake, *The Early History*, 177; Bolles and Williams, *The Rogerenes*, 130-31; Greene, *The Development of Religious Liberty*, 161; Caulkins, *History of New London*, 204.

urdays as his day of rest. For working on the Congregational Sabbath, Rogers and his family initially paid five shillings apiece, but that fine incrementally increased to £5 by 1677. In that same year, court records indicate that John, James, and Joseph Rogers joined forces with those outside of their family. Richard Smith and Joseph Horton were listed alongside the Rogers men in charges showing nonattendance at church.[16]

Rogers's zeal for the Sabbatarian doctrine landed him the pastorate of the newly formed New London Seventh Day Baptist Church in 1675. For two years Rogers dutifully preached every week to his congregants and also organized protests against the Sunday Sabbath. Rogers spent a fair amount of time studying the Scriptures to properly teach his flock, and local sectarians noticed his commitment to personal meditations and extended periods of prayer. None of his parishioners would have guessed that during these private moments, Rogers started doubting certain Sabbatarian doctrines. First, Rogers became troubled by the Sabbatarian denial of the Trinity. Further, the more he delved into Scriptural interpretation, Rogers became convinced that a strict adherence to a seventh-day Sabbath was contrary to Jesus' exposition of this ritual. Rogers still held that most of the Sabbatarian teachings were valid because he was called "out of darkness" through these tenets. Questions regarding the Trinity and Sabbath, however, distressed him deeply.[17]

In the midst of these confusing times, Rogers became acquainted with two religious dissenters who further challenged his Sabbatarian beliefs. William Edmundson, a Quaker from Ireland, arrived in New London in 1676 and befriended Rogers and his parishioners. Edmundson found this group "very tender and loving" and even spent time with them "in fervent prayer to God." Yet, Edmundson engaged Rogers in long talks into the night about potential errors of Sabbatarianism, and Rogers must have been especially confounded since the usually loquacious leader "was silent."[18] Also, John Liveen, a business partner from Barbados, added to Rogers's

---

[16] Bolles and Williams, *The Rogerenes*, 142; William G. McLoughlin, *New England Dissent, 1630-1833: The Baptists and the Separation of Church and State* (Cambridge: Harvard University Press, 1971), 1:251.

[17] John Rogers, *An Epistle to the Churches of Christ call'd Quakers; And Another Epistle to the Seventh Day Baptists, with Several Theological Essays* (New York: William Bradford, 1705), 38.

[18] William Edmundson, *A Journal of the Life, Travels, Sufferings, and Labour of Love in the Work of the Ministry, of that Worthy Elder and Faithful Servant of Jesus Christ, William Edmundson, Who Departed this Life, the Thirty-first of the Sixth Month, 1712, 3rd ed.* (Dublin: Christopher Bentham, 1820), 109-15.

doubts. Liveen subscribed to a strain of Anabaptism and challenged Rogers to reassess his Sabbatarian views.[19] These men left lingering doubts in Rogers's already unsettled mind.[20]

The following year Rogers decided to break off from the Sabbatarians entirely. On November 24, 1677, the day of his sister-in-law's baptism, Rogers publicly denounced Thomas Hiscox and Samuel Hubbard, leaders of the Newport Sabbatarians, by refusing to comply with their decision to baptize Elizabeth Rogers in private. Simon Bradstreet, the pastor of the First Congregational Church in New London, sanctioned the baptism as long as the Sabbatarians quietly convened among themselves. Hiscox and Hubbard agreed to this compromise, but Rogers refused and took it upon himself to publicly baptize his sister-in-law at Winthrop's Cove. This baptism marked the official end of his tenure as a Sabbatarian.[21]

Though Rogers's days as a Sabbatarian came to an end in 1677, his commitment to sectarian piety was just beginning. At this fateful November baptism, Rogers started his own religious sect, the Rogerenes. From the outset, Rogers worked hard to define the theological framework behind this movement. The fundamental doctrines of this sect were surprisingly orthodox, such as their belief in the Trinity, commitment to Calvinist doctrine in matters of salvation, and prominence given to Scripture. Rogerenes subscribed to pacifism and faith healing, which were reminiscent of Quaker traditions; and like the Baptists, they practiced full-immersion baptism. Rogerenes, however, veered off on a new trajectory altogether as they announced that any concept of a Sabbath should be annulled and that the Lord's Supper should only be observed in the evenings.[22]

---

[19] Caulkins, *History of New London*, 222-25.

[20] A good reference for colonial trade, including sectarian actions, is Bernard Bailyn, *The New England Merchants in the Seventeenth Century* (New York: Harper & Row, 1955) and Mark Valeri, *Heavenly Merchandize: How Religion Shaped Commerce in Puritan America* (Princeton: Princeton University Press, 2010), esp. 5–10.

[21] Bolles and Williams, T*he Rogerenes,* 146-47; Brinton, "The Rogerenes," 7.

[22] Blake, *The Early History*, 179-80; Greene, T*he Development of Religious Liberty*, 162; McLoughlin, *New England Dissent*, 1:251; John Rogers, *John Rogers a Servant of Jesus Christ, to any of the Flock of Christ that may be scattered among the Churches of New-England, Greeting, 4th ed.* (Norwich: n.p., 1776).

Rogerene Families

This sect, from the beginning obscure and precarious, received some legitimacy because of the Rogers name. John Rogers hailed from a well-regarded New London family who had great prestige, wealth, and influence. The Rogers patriarch, James Rogers, had close connections with Connecticut Governor, John Winthrop, Jr., and he joined the Rogerenes soon after their inception. Many of John Rogers's other family members who had followed him into Sabbatarianism continued to follow him into this newly formed sect.

With the majority of his family members in support of his sect, John Rogers used his money and influence to pioneer a new religion. The rate list for the ministry tax in 1664 indicates that James Rogers had nearly double the taxable property of any other inhabitant in New London, an estimated £548, and his tax rate was £7, 19s, 10d.[23] With his sizable holdings, Rogers did his best to secure profitable futures for his children, such as his purchase of Richard Blinman's farm for his son John and a farm in Waterford for his son Joseph.[24]

James Rogers's sizable estate is also documented through the bitter legal disputes between the Rogers children upon his passing. The Rogers patriarch must have known the temperament of his children, for in his will he repeated several times his desire that his children "not to fall out" of good standing with one another and that they remain "Contend" with whatever lot was given to them. He asked that his children's love for one another prove greater than their love for "the Estate" he left to them. Explicitly, he asked that there be "no Lawing among my Children before Earthly judges," but if contention should arise, disputes should "be Ended by Lott." Sadly, his children did not respect their father's wishes.[25]

Though James Rogers's death in February 1688 initially left the Rogers children with an amicable division of land and goods, thereafter an acrimonious struggle ensued between certain family members. Elizabeth Beebe, James Rogers's daughter, was unhappy with her three cows

---
[23] Caulkins, *History of New London*, 152.
[24] Bolles and Williams, *The Rogerenes*, 123-24.
[25] Connecticut State Library, Private Controversies, Series 2, VI:132b, c.

and wanted a "Negro girl and certain utensils" in addition to her inheritance. Her siblings, John and Bathsheba Rogers, attempted to block this request with a countersuit. Further, Joseph Rogers insisted that John Rogers had promised to put him in charge of their father's house but had reneged on this promise. Bathshua Rogers, daughter of James Rogers, Jr., vouched for Joseph Rogers further complicating matters. These were just a few of many examples where the Rogerses were in heated legal battles with one another over their sizable holdings. With much land and many goods, the Rogerses had a great deal about which to squabble.[26] Interestingly, many of these pecuniary matters largely did not affect the family's support of the Rogerene movement.

While alive, James Rogers was able to offer significant aid to his children through the respect he received from the community as well as through his wealth. Rogers became a New London inhabitant in 1657 and was elected one of three commissioners in 1660. In May 1660, the General Court granted New London one assistant and three commissioners who held full power to oversee a variety of local needs. Some of these duties entailed making sure that fenced-borders were observed, keeping the children educated, maintaining the meetinghouse, and controlling all matters related to neighboring and close-by Native Americans. James Rogers was one of the first three commissioners to be chosen to this post, and in 1664 he, along with Ensigne Averye, was called upon to manage all affairs between New London and Saybrook. These appointments highlighted James Rogers's respectable standing in the community. Moreover, church membership was a key component in obtaining community respect, and James Rogers joined the church in the early 1670s.[27] His wife had joined the Congregational Church of New London in 1670 and Rogers followed suit "not long after."[28]

Even before James Rogers became a visible saint of New London, he contributed much to church affairs. He, along with "Levt. Smith, Cary Latham, John Smith, and William Hough," were "appointed [by the church] to goe to Mr. Buckley" and assume the task of "settling in"

---

[26] Connecticut State Library, Private Controversies, Series 1.
[27] Church membership was thought to be comprised of no more than five to fifteen percent of the colonial population. In fact, American churches are thought to have had the fewest members in the early to mid-seventeenth century when compared to churches around the world. William Warren Sweet, "The American Colonial Environment and Religious Liberty," *Church History*, (no. 4, 1935): 52.
[28] Caulkins, *History of New London*, 90-92, 144, 166.

their new pastor on January 15, 1664.[29] Apparently things did not turn out well with Mr. Buckley since he departed the year after. His reasons for leaving are "obscurely intimated" and his short tenure meant that "no great formality" was needed for his release.

The year after, a new pastoral candidate, Rev. Nathaniel Brewster of Brookhaven Long Island, was scouted. On July 10, 1665, "Mr. James Rogers" was asked to "goe in the behalfe of the towne to Mr. Brewster" to enquire if he would be their minister. Specifically, Rogers was charged to "give [Brewster] a call and to know whether he will come to us to be our minister." There is no further mention of Brewster, which could mean one of two things. Either Brewster did not want the job, or Rogers had an unfavorable opinion of him. The suggestion that Rogers could thwart the candidacy of the town pastor implies that he held a significant amount of respect and power within New London.[30]

As most moneyed and influential men, James Rogers did his best to provide advantages for his children and connect them with other affluent members of society. In 1670, when John Rogers was just twenty-two years old, his father contracted for his marriage to Elizabeth Griswold, daughter of Matthew and Anna Griswold of Saybrook.[31] As with most upscale dowries, the marriage settlement between the Rogers and Griswolds was generous, including a spacious house replete with a twenty square-foot living room, imported furniture, ample livestock, and ready servants. The newlyweds had sufficient "leisure" time to pursue personal interests, which included extensive Bible studies and discussions about religious matters. It seemed the two were well matched in all respects.[32]

Beyond securing favorable marriage contracts, James Rogers also endeavored to include his children in affairs that were deemed important by the community. One of the New Londoners' major concerns revolved around the Native Americans who posed a threat to their safety and wellbeing. The Narragansetts and Pequots were especially formidable dangers to New London inhabitants in the decades after settlement. When James Rogers was called upon to protect his community from

---

[29] Ibid., 136.
[30] Ibid., 138.
[31] Bolles and Williams, *The Rogerenes*, 124.
[32] Briton, "The Rogerenes," 6-7.

Native Americans, he seized this opportunity to enlist his son, Samuel Rogers, to take part. On October 28, 1675, seven New Londoners were chosen to fortify their town, and James Rogers recruited Samuel Rogers to be a part of this group. This post provided Samuel Rogers with an opportunity to display to New Londoners his qualities of leadership and dependability.[33]

Even if it meant that his prestige and honor in the community would be compromised, the Rogers patriarch ardently supported John Rogers's sectarianism. His first allegiance was to his children, and James Rogers willingly renounced his Congregational membership and became a Rogerene soon after the sect began. To equate the Rogerses' wealth and prestige to the Rogerene cause is appropriate because many of John Rogers's family members, especially his venerated father, were baptized as Rogerenes and became committed members. In fact, considerable attention was given when a Rogers did not accept Rogerene doctrine or left the Rogerene fold. Such was the case when Jonathan Rogers refused to work on the Sabbath and did not subscribe to faith-healing practices, two important aspects of Rogerene policy. A majority of the Rogerses wholeheartedly pledged their allegiance to the Rogerene movement and dedicated themselves, as well as their wealth and social connections, to this sectarian cause. Soon after their conversions, however, the Rogerses' prominence was sorely tested as they continued on a dissenting path and undertook the ambitious task of redefining the Puritan way.

Fortunately for the Rogers Family, they did not stand alone in this dissenting movement. They shouldered the majority of the responsibilities, but other Rogerene leaders outside of the founding family also brought a measure of affluence and respect to the dissenting movement. Surnames that have been prominent within the Rogerene leadership were Beeby, Bolles, Culver, and Waterhouse, all well-regarded families in New London. Jacob Waterhouse was one of the first planters in New London, and he was awarded "six ackers for an house lot next to John Stubens" in 1647. Stubens (or Stebbins) owned a plot of land northwest of Governor Winthrop's property, which meant that Waterhouse, by propinquity, was well situated. In the year 1649, New Londoners were

---

[33] Caulkins, *History of New London*, 182-83.

corporately and principally concerned about their livestock and arable lands, and Waterhouse and Stubens were chosen as overseers of these valuable assets. Also, Waterhouse was recognized as the owner of the only ox in town. No other ox was mentioned on five rate lists in 1651.[34]

The Beeby brothers, John, Samuel, and Thomas, most likely arrived in New London in 1651, when there was a surge in settlement. Samuel Beeby might have arrived a few years earlier, perhaps with his brother John, in service to Governor Winthrop. Samuel Beeby, husband of Elizabeth Rogers, owned land in New London at a place known as Fog Plain. He, along with his brothers, also owned land in Goshen, which was near the estate of his father-in-law, James Rogers.[35]

Edward Culver was awarded a house lot in New London and a farm in Mystic on November 20, 1652. A few years later in 1661, his eldest son, John Culver, arrived in town and was granted a small portion of land near the waterside. On May 5, 1662 "Goodman Culver" was chosen "by the towne" for "the making of bread and bruing of beere for the publicke good." Culver's duty of baking bread must have brought him into conversation with James Rogers, who was the town's most prominent baker. On May 7, 1663 John Culver was chosen "to drum Saboth days and as formerly for meetings," an appointment indicating the favor he had garnered from his fellow inhabitants of New London. Thomas Bolles augmented the respectability of Rogerene leadership when in 1688 he arrived in New London from Wells, in Maine, with the ability to buy a sizeable amount of property.[36]

Of course not all Rogerenes were rich or well connected, and this was especially the case for the rank and file. Although the Rogerene leadership boasted of men with illustrious careers or respectable birthrights, regular Rogerene members were from varied backgrounds. All members had opportunities to rise within the Rogerene ranks through their dedication and zeal, but only men of respectable birthright led the Rogerene movement. There were wealthy members, such as Thomas Young, an affluent New London citizen who was baptized by John Rogers on November 6, 1692. But there were also Rogerenes who were

---
[34] Ibid.
[35] Ibid., 70, 95.
[36] Ibid., 134-35, 146.

disenfranchised, socially and politically, from the larger society. Japhet, a Native American, was a servant to James Rogers and followed his master's lead into the Rogerene fold. In 1685 John Rogers was fined £5 for baptizing an African-American woman into the Rogerene faith. John Jackson, a free black resident in New London, endured stripes and jail time for the Rogerene cause. Widows, merchants, and yeoman farmers also added into the mix of Rogerenes.

Sectarianism in New London

As founder of the Rogerenes, John Rogers assumed all ministerial offices, such as preaching the gospel, baptizing converts, and administering communion, but later he passed some of these responsibilities to others within the fold. Although the first Rogerene converts consisted solely of family members, the sect grew fairly quickly within a few years and included New Londoners of various social backgrounds. By 1680, the Rogerenes boasted of a small but committed group consisting of several dozen people. At their height between 1700 and 1720, the Rogerenes had nearly two hundred members residing in New London, which made them the largest sect in the region.[37] Rogers was wary of a large following and actually preferred to lead a small group. He believed false prophets "are always the greatest Number" because the masses of people unwittingly follow after them.[38] For Rogers, his small numbers only confirmed the authenticity of his teachings.

Soon after the sect arose, Rogers led his disciples in formal protests against the Congregational order. In June 1678, James Rogers, Sr. and his sons, John and James, entered the New London meetinghouse and took their seats, which must have been in one of the most prominent sections since the elder James Rogers was the largest taxpayer in town. The three Rogers men stood up in the middle of service and started objecting to the First-Day Sabbath. They were immediately taken to prison, put on trial, and fined £5.[39] Interestingly, these histrionic protests were undergirded by much thought and theological explanation. Rogers spent a fair amount of time and ink sharing his

[37] McLoughlin, *New England Dissent*, I:250.
[38] Rogers, *An Epistle to the Churches of Christ call'd Quakers*, iv.
[39] Bolles, *The Rogerenes*, 152.

views on what made up the true Church and from which beliefs it derived legitimacy. From the outset, Rogers made it clear that he was not creating merely another sect. He believed that he was reclaiming what the disciples of Jesus had started in the first century.

In fact, Rogers did not call his followers "Rogerenes," although they are referred to this name in academic work so as not to confuse the reader. Rogers simply called himself and his followers "Christians." The word "Rogerene" first appeared in 1754 and then gained wide usage after the historian Isaac Backus used this term in 1777.[40] Before then, the usual titles to identify this group were "John Rogers & his Crew" and "John Rogers & Company."[41]

The fact remains, however, that Rogers did create another sect; and, ironically, he stated plainly "if we will be Christ's Disciples, we must have no Respect to Sects." Rogers referenced the Scriptures when, in the Apostle Paul's time, sectarians segregated themselves under the leadership of various men, such as Apollos and Cephas, and created strife due to their doctrinal differences. Rogers looked at his current state of affairs and believed New Englanders were wrongfully following in these sectarians' footsteps when "saith one, The *Papists* is the right Way, another the *Church of England*, another is for the Presbyterian, another for the Quaker, another for the *Baptists*." Rogers stated that Christ was larger than sectarianism, and argued rhetorically "is [Christ] not a Man of a seamless Garment?" He answered his own question in the affirmative and further maintained, "we see the Members of Christ are not Sectaries, but are united together, in a perfect Bond of Love and Unity." Further, he stated that the true mark of Christianity was found in the "Spirit of Love, that came from God, the Fountain of Love, who hath shed it in our Hearts, by the Holy Ghost that dwelleth in us."[42]

This nebulous term had concrete meanings for the Rogerenes, who believed that love expressed itself in harmonious interactions with

---

[40] Jan Schenk Grosskopf, "Family, Religion, and Disorder: The Rogerenes of New London, 1676-1726," *Connecticut History* 40 (2001): 206.

[41] Joshua Hempstead, D*iary of Joshua Hempstead of New London, Connecticut: Covering a Period of Forty-Seven Years from September 1711 to November 1758* (New London: The New London Historical Society, 1901), 55, 91, 97, 108, 162.

[42] John Rogers, A*n Epistle Sent from God to the World, containing the Best News that ever the World Heard. And transcribed by John Rogers, a Servant of Jesus Christ* (New York: Printed for Elisha Stanbury, 1720/1), 25.

all people, including those of differing faiths. There was a group of people, however, that Rogers condemned as heretical, and they were the Congregationalists. What place the Congregationalist beyond the scope of redemption for Rogers were not doctrinal issues, but their laws and policies that seemingly blocked true fellowship and goodwill amongst New Londoners. Rogerenes accused the Congregationalists of purposefully keeping New Englanders in ignorance despite their wills by undercutting civic and religious dialogue. Rogers and his son, John Rogers Jr., surmised that "there are many thousands of grown Persons in this Colony, that for want of opportunity to be informed in the Principles of other Sects, remain so ignorant." They were not given the opportunity to assess for themselves what is right and wrong religion, and, thus, "know no difference between the Church of England and the *Papists*, nor between the *Quaker* and the *Baptists*, but esteem each couple to be alike." Rogerenes believed that Congregationalists intentionally kept the masses in the dark by outlawing the spreading of any other belief in their bid to retain a monopoly on religion.[43]

Rogers vowed to contravene these "manmade laws" so that he might abide to a higher standard. He believed that the unity of love, as spoken of in the Scriptures, did not prevent one denomination from debating or reproving another; and, further, he adhered to the notion that discord in theology could peacefully be discussed and need not be points of irreconcilable tension between sectarians. For example, Rogers spent considerable time meeting with and writing to Quakers on topics he found problematic, as he believed the Society of Friends erroneously adopted some biblical principles that needed further illumination. Differences in doctrine, however, did not prevent Rogers from embracing them as "Christ's Disciples" and "Christian Reader[s]." In his *Epistle to the Churches of Christ call'd Quakers*, he exhorted Quakers and Rogerenes alike to regard themselves as "God's People in Love" and remain in the "Unity and Fellowship" of Christ's body.[44]

Although Rogers laid claim to the true church, he endeavored to commune with those outside his fold. Before Rogers formed an opinion of any sect, he took the time to fully acquaint himself with their doc-

---

[43] Ibid., vi-vii.
[44] Rogers, *An Epistle to the Churches of Christ call'd Quakers*, 1.

trines and practices. Such was also the case for his son and successor, John Rogers, Jr. and other surviving members. Rogers encouraged people of all faiths to read as much as they could about opposing faiths. He contended that a secure believer did not need to isolate himself from all other beliefs but should all the more be educated in competing theologies. Without such knowledge, true believers could not speak intelligently and persuasively to people outside their fold. And without such knowledge, there would be no avenue to compare the false church with the true church.

The breadth of knowledge that Rogers held about his own and variant faiths around him reveals a man who understood the depths and nuances of Scripture. The following chapters will tell of Rogers's adherence to the fundamentals of the Bible and how these ideas manifested in New London. Rogers's rationale for each of his theological pillars and actions are indeed surprisingly supported through both Old and New Testament passages. The many demonstrations that have earned Rogers's a place along with fringe religious groups need to be contextualized in his own words, which in turn were influenced greatly by the Scriptures. Rogers's life clearly indicates that sectarianism did not always equate a subordination or ignorance of the holy texts. Indeed, the opposite holds true for this sectarian who was radical in his adherence to the Bible.

SOLA SCRIPTURA

Chapter 2

The Sabbath

True Rest

John Rogers and his "crew" caused a "great disturbance" by "behaving themselves in such a frantic manner as if possessed with a diabolical spirit, so affrighting and amazing that several women swooned and fainted away" in the New London meetinghouse.[1] Soon thereafter, on April 14, 1685, Judges Fitch, Avery, and Wetherell ordered John Rogers to pay £5 and be "whipped fifteen lashes" for disturbing the Congregational Sabbath.[2] Such punishments, however, failed to deter John Rogers and his followers from intruding upon Sunday worship. To Rogers, nothing reeked more of pomp and pageantry than the Congregational Sabbath, and he and his followers made sure to exhibit their disdain for this manmade tradition set up by the "false church."[3]

These riotous acts deeply offended the Congregationalists, who responded with heavy-handed reprisals. Although the intrusion upon worship incited the ire of Congregational leaders, the theology and Scriptural justifications behind the Rogerenes' actions enraged them just the same. John Rogers argued that the Congregationalists "bound [themselves] to unscriptural Rites in Religion" by the "Addition and Diminution" of "the Canon."[4] Rogers searched the Scrip-

---

[1] Rogers's "crew" that day happened to be comprised of James Rogers, Jr., Samuel Beebee, Jr., and Joanna Way. Although historians use the term "Rogerene" to describe this sect, colonists did not use this name to identify Rogers's followers until 1725. Until then, the Rogerenes were called "John Rogers & his Crew" or "John Rogers & Company" according to Joshua Hempstead, *Diary of Joshua Hempstead of New London, Connecticut: Covering a Period of Forty-Seven Years from September 1711 to November 1758* (New London: The New London Historical Society, 1901), 55, 91, 97, 108, 162.
[2] New London Town Rec., lib. 4, folio 46 in Frances Manwaring Caulkins, *History of New London, Connecticut: From the First Survey of the Coast in 1612, to 1860* (New London: H.D. Utley, 1895), 211. The judges also ordered that Rogers's followers be whipped, but the number of lashes is unrecorded.
[3] Caulkins, *History of New London, Connecticut*, 212.
[4] John Rogers, *An answer to a Book Intituled, The Lords Day proved to be the Christian Sabbath &c. By B. Wadsworth, A.M. Pastor of a Church in Boston. And also, An Answer to a Pamphlet, Intituled Thesis concerning the Sabbath. As Also, Some Part of what hath passed through the General Courts in Connecticut Colony, relating to the Sabbath. As Also, Some Court Sentences in that Colony, by John Rogers* (Boston: n.p., 1721), 9.

tures and found nowhere the type of Sabbath that the Congregationalists advocated. In fact, he argued that "Christ has no regard to the [Sabbath] Day" and that only a "false church" would force an entire community to observe a "manmade tradition" like the Sunday Sabbath.[5]

The stakes were high in this debate, as both sides believed that God's favor and wrath rested upon properly understanding this rite. Thomas Shepard well articulated the Congregationalists' stance when he stated:

> our children, servants, strangers who are within our gates, are apt to profane the Sabbath; we are therefore to improve our power over them for God, in restraining them from sin, and in constraining them (as far as we can) to the holy observance of the rest of the Sabbath, lest God impute their sins to us, who had power (as Eli in the like case) to restrain them and did not; and so our families and consciences be stained with their guilt and blood.[6]

Under this type of covenant described by Shepard, God promised prosperity and peace in exchange for a people's external obedience. If any member of a community failed to comply with the given edicts, the entire "nation," or community, would expect the withdrawal of God's provisions and protection. Even worse, perhaps God's wrath and fury could be unleashed upon a disobedient people. As a result, Congregationalists were invested in securing the obedience of all inhabitants to ensure their own blessings from God. It was no surprise, then, that the Congregationalists felt personally affected when John Rogers claimed a different position on the keeping of a Sunday-Sabbath.[7]

The Sabbath was a vital aspect of religious life in colonial times, whatever the denomination. The ample number of sermons, treatises, debates, and commentary devoted to the Sabbath reflects the importance colonists ascribed to weekly rest. This widely discussed topic held significant meaning for most faiths, and New Londoners largely subscribed to either a Saturday or Sunday Sabbath. Different camps expended much energy debating one another on this sacred concept of rest, hop-

---

[5] Ibid., 19.
[6] Thomas Shepard, *The Works of Thomas Shepard* (Boston: Doctrinal Tract and Book Society, 1853), III:263.
[7] A basic but helpful reference for all things related to the Congregational Sabbath is Alice Morse Earle's *The Sabbath in Puritan New England* (New York: Charles Scribner's Sons, 1891).

ing to persuade dissidents to see a truer exposition of the Scriptures.

The Congregationalists were particularly prolific in their writings defending a First-Day Sabbath, which they believed was instrumental in honoring their state covenant with God.[8] Sabbatarians vigorously defended a Saturday Sabbath by citing Jewish traditions and the Ten Commandments. John Rogers weighed in on this dispute by abolishing the concept of a Sabbath altogether. He claimed that observing the Sabbath on any day was contrary to the heart of the gospel. Rogers still believed in the assembly of like-minded believers and communal worship, but he could not support the notion of consecrating any one day as holy.

Many of John Rogers's thoughts on the Sabbath were formulated during his tenure as a Sabbatarian. During his Sabbatarian days, Rogers had close fellowship with the Newport Sabbatarians, who were largely influenced by English Sabbatarian Stephen Mumford.[9] While a Sabbatarian, Rogers believed that the Sabbath could be observed on a day other than Sunday. Later, when Rogers led his own sect in Sabbath demonstrations, his actions were reminiscent of his Sabbatarian days, but his theology was completely different. When John Rogers broke from the Newport Sabbatarians and constructed his own Sabbatarian laws in 1677, he made this bold move through his understanding of key passages from the Bible regarding this topic. Rogers's rationale for subscribing to a working Sunday Sabbath stemmed from his zealous desire to understand the Scriptures accurately.

Rogerene doctrine held that communal worship could be held on any day of the week, and this assembly did not impede all normal activities thereafter. As to which day communal worship is to be held, a designation should be left to each individual body of believers as a matter of preference and convenience. Rogers stated that "I have no where read in the Books

---

[8] The state covenant was also known as the family covenant or church covenant. This was different from an individual's covenant with God, which was known as the covenant of grace.

[9] As members of the Bell Lane Sabbatarian Church in England, Mumford and his wife, Ann, faced persecution, and similarly other English Sabbatarians were harassed for observing their holy day on Saturday rather than Sunday. Their situation in Old England was not unlike their co-religionists in Newport, who were treated with floggings, imprisonments and even hangings. The interregnum years were a time of adversity for Sabbatarians in England and not much changed after King Charles I was restored to the monarchy in 1660. In light of such persecution, the Mumfords left England and were documented as the first Sabbatarians to reach American soil in 1665. After landing in Newport they helped found the Seventh Day Baptist Church of Newport in 1671. They had begun to meet a few years earlier but the church was officially established in 1671.

of the New Testament, that we are commanded to keep one Day more holy than another" and therefore chose Sunday as his preferential day of worship.[10] This was undoubtedly in opposition to Sabbatarian principles rather than in compliance with New London law.[11] The Congregationalists were not pleased with Rogers's choice to worship on Sunday, however, for the Rogerenes believed that the Sabbath did not prohibit work, play, or any other normal activity to be performed on the day of rest.[12]

Rogers's treatise on the Sabbath was largely in response to *The Lords Day proved to be the Christian Sabbath, &c.*, by Benjamin Wadsworth, a leading Congregational minister. When Wadsworth argued that "The Apostle doth not oppose the keeping one Day in a week holy to God,"[13] Rogers responded by saying, "It is not what the Apostle doth not oppose, but what the Apostle commands." Rogers argued for a perpetual holiness that exceeded worship punctuated by weekly rituals, and he maintained that terminating the Congregational Sabbath would provide a deeper measure of devotion and rest than the current system bestowed.[14]

Identifying the beneficiary of the Sabbath proved crucial to Rogers's annulment of the holy day. If God were the main beneficiary of the Sabbath, as Rogers purported that the Congregationalists believed, naturally man should adjust their schedules to worship and venerate the holy deity. If men, however, were the recipients of Sabbatical activity, as the Rogerenes believed, New England's notion of the holy day needed to be radically revamped. Rogerenes believed that the Sabbath was instituted for the profit of man, and, specifically, the goal was to alleviate the burdens of day-to-day activities that taxed the body and spirit. Therefore, it made no sense to the Rogerenes that the Congregational Sabbath provided anything but rest. Laden with hyper-religious obligations and rituals, New Englanders were far from refreshed after an arduous Sunday of intense physical and spiritual exertion. Although Congregationalists ap-

---

[10] Rogers, *An answer to a Book Intituled, The Lords Day proved to be the Christian Sabbath*, 4.

[11] In the previous chapter, I discuss how John Rogers became a Sabbatarian but left this denomination in 1677 due to doctrinal differences. His departure from the Sabbatarians was not on the best terms, so it's not surprising that Rogers would choose a non-Saturday as the Rogerene day of worship.

[12] Caulkins, *History of New London, Connecticut*, 205.

[13] Benjamin Wadsworth, *The Lord's Day, Proved to be the Christian Sabbath. Or Reasons Showing Why the First Day of the Week (called the Lord's Day) should be kept holy as the Christian Sabbath* (Boston: B. Green, 1720), 5.

[14] Rogers, *An Answer to a Book Intituled, The Lords Day Proved to be the Christian Sabbath*, 4.

plied the concept of rest in the realms of commercial labor and recreational practices, true rest eluded the reach of most New Londoners. Certainly, multiple visits to the meetinghouse, sometimes through snow, hail and storm, and protracted services, often requiring a rigid posture and intense concentration, were antithetical to the notion of rest and rejuvenation.

Further, Rogerenes believed that the Congregationalists' adherence to a weekly Sunday Sabbath brought idolatry into the land by forcing New Englanders to worship images rather than Christ. Rogers stated that the Sabbath was nothing more than a sign of the true and eternal rest to come, but he argued that the Congregationalists made the Sabbath the object of worship. Instead of assessing the Sabbath as merely a sign, Congregationalists deemed the Sabbath itself holy, which was heretical in Rogers's view. The Sabbath was only sacred because of who it represented and not because it held any intrinsic value on its own. The Sabbath, then, was merely a "shadow" of Christ and not Christ Himself, according to Rogers; to exalt the "sign" rather than the "Substance" was nothing short of idolatry.

Even in Old Testament times, Rogers argued, those who understood the Sabbath believed that it was made for man and not man for the Sabbath. Rogers believed that there were justifiable times when God's people could disregard the Sabbath without impunity because the point of rest was to facilitate the welfare of believers. He pointed to biblical references that revealed circumstances that could call for work, travel, or healing on the Sabbath but that Pharisaical leaders did not accept any exceptions to the rule. Though "Christ testifieth, That the Priests prophaned the Sabbath in the Temple, and yet were blameless," the ritualists held fast to the law without pondering why the rule even existed. Rogers condemned the Pharisees of the past as lost in their religiosity and their Congregationalist counterparts, in his present, of failing to rationally think through and grasp the motives behind the Sabbath.[15]

Rogers contended that man was in search of an eternal Sabbath and not a temporal one; and that true rest came from casting humanity's burdens upon the shoulders of Jesus, who alone is strong and gracious

---

[15] John Rogers, *An Epistle to the Churches of call'd Quakers; And another epistle to the Seventh Day Baptists, with several Theological Essays* (New York: William Bradford, 1705), 55-57, 60.

enough to carry man's sins and infirmities.[16] Rogerenes understood that sin was not an act but a disposition, and that no amount of sacrifice, penance or good works could diminish the fall of mankind. Man needed so much more than one day solely dedicated to worship to garner God's favor. Rogerenes balked at the notion that such a small pittance could be considered sufficient. They believed that the true Sabbath could only be accessed by accepting Jesus as the Messiah and believing that "Christ had finished his work of Redemption for us." After the death and resurrection of Christ, "he entred into his rest, having ceased from his own works, as God did from his" and is now able to offer true rest to those who believe in Christ's redemptive power.[17] Furthermore, Rogers argued that true worship should be continual rather than concentrated in a single day, "For they that worship him now in Gospel Times, *must worship him in Spirit and in Truth,* in their inward Man, without Regard to Time or Place."[18]

When the Sabbath was instituted in the Old Testament, it served as a foreshadowing of the true Sabbath to come and was never meant to be observed perpetually. In the days of animal sacrifices, people conducted rituals to appease God's wrath, and one of those ceremonial acts was reserving a holy day for worship. The most elaborate of rituals could never undo man's sinful nature, and, if anything, pointed to the need of a greater sacrifice. Thus, Rogers argued that the death of Jesus, the sacrificial Lamb of the world, was the only sacrifice capable of reconciling fallen man to a holy God, and that the offering of time, energies, and productivity were insufficient sacrifices, just as the blood of bulls and goats could not compare with the atoning blood of Jesus.

Turning to Exodus 31 as proof, Rogers made his defense: "In the 13th Verse saith the Lord, *Verily my Sabbath ye shall keep, for it is a Sign between me and you. It is a Sign between me and the Children of Israel.* And a Sign Is not the thing signified by it, no more than the *Shadow* of a thing is the *Substance.*"[19] In Rogers's view New Londoners needed to better understand the context in which the Sabbath

---

[16] Rogers, *An Answer to a Book Intituled, The Lords Day proved to be the Christian Sabbath*, 16.
[17] John Rogers, *A Mid-Night Cry from the Temple of God to the Ten Virgins Slumbering and Sleeping, Awake, Awake, Arise, and gird your Loyns, and trim your Lamps, for behold the Bridegroom cometh, go ye therefore out to meet him* (New London: Green, 1822 [original published 1705, New York]), 143.
[18] Rogers, *An Answer to a Book Intituled, The Lords Day proved to be the Christian Sabbath*, 5.
[19] Ibid., 6.

was originally mandated. After Moses had successfully led the Israelites out of Egyptian bondage, the Sabbath was instituted as a reminder of God's faithfulness. Rogers made clear that the deliverance was "from a Temporal Bondage, so the sign of it was a Temporal Rest." In Rogers's time, believers of the New Covenant sought redemption from something much greater than an oppressive Pharaoh or Egyptian army; men and women sought deliverance from their own sinful natures.[20]

The substance of the temporal sign was the only avenue to such freedom, according to Rogers. If the substance already appeared, as Rogerenes believed to be made manifest in the embodiment of Christ, then the sign was now unnecessary. In Old Testament times, "the 7th-Day Sabbath was a Sign under the first Covenant" and ceased when the second covenant was "fulfilled by Christ, who was the substance" of the sign.[21] Just as a figure trumps its own shadow and cannot replace the image, the sign is inferior to the substance in integrity and form. Rogers could not understand why Congregationalists insisted on embracing the symbol when its manifestation had arrived.[22] Many people were unable to come to this true rest because of their unbelief, Rogerenes argued. They could not see that rightful work is the work of faith, not of physical labor. "A Christian must enter into God's Sabbath, by faith, for by faith we come to enter into Adam's innocent state, for he entred into God's Sabbath."[23] Rogers echoed the Apostle Paul, who exhorted fellow believers to discontinue their steadfast adherence to the old law of works "to that which is abolished.[24]

While Rogers rejected the idea of reserving an entire day for worship altogether, he wanted to clarify how to properly conduct the Sabbath instituted in the Old Testament. "For we find by Record of Scripture, that in Christ's time they were very zealous in the Observation of the Seventh Day Sabbath, having a very plain Commandment for it, and often judged our Savior as being guilty of the Breach of it," Rogers taught. In this lengthy sentence, Rogers pointed out that the Sab-

---

[20] Rogers, *An Epistle to the Churches of Christ call'd Quakers*, 60.
[21] Ibid., 61-62.
[22] Rogers believed that certain signs still remained and their manifestation (or substance) would appear at the second coming of Christ. Namely, two such signs were baptism and the Lord's Supper.
[23] Rogers, *A Mid-Night-Cry from the Temple of God*, 138.
[24] Ibid., 145.

bath had always been observed on the seventh day, which is Saturday, during Old Testament times. Further, during Christ's time, this tradition persisted. Hence, although the Sabbath should no longer exist, Rogers believed that those who insisted on its practice should observe it on the *intended* day. It was both that Congregationalists insisted on a Sabbath and the way they instituted this day that agitated John Rogers.[25]

Rogers believed that when the Sabbath was observed in Old Testament times, Scripture explicitly made clear that the holy day should be on the seven-day (Saturday) and not the first (Sunday).[26] Rogers plainly stated, "The Acts of the *Apostles* was written many Years after Christ's Ascension into Heaven, and calls no other Day the Sabbath, but the seventh Day of the Week" and that he could "find no other Weekly Sabbath instituted in the holy Scriptures, or any other Weekly Day commanded, called or kept for a Sabbath throughout the Bible."[27] Scouring the Scriptures, he dutifully outlined every mention of the Sabbath in the Old and New Testaments and argued why Saturday was always indicated as the intended day of rest. Moreover, Rogers outlined the many New Testament passages that displayed various forms of work being performed on Sunday. For example, Rogers pointed to the empty tomb as the prime instance of Christ having instituted work on Sunday. On the day of Christ's resurrection, the Angel of the Lord commanded Mary Magdalene to travel and inform the disciples of the resurrection. Travel, except to and from church, on the Sabbath was considered an offense in biblical and colonial days, and Rogers made clear that the Angel of the Lord would never have directed Mary Magdalene to purposefully travel and relay this message on the resurrection day if Sunday were to be the Sabbath.

There were always exceptions to the rule and even Christ dictated that travel was allowable on the Sabbath on certain occasions. These exceptions, however, should be rare rather than recurrent, as was the case in many biblical examples. To further his point, Rogers pointed to other biblical illustrations in which Christ advocated travel on Sunday. There were enough examples of such travel that Rogers argued it must have been an allowable statute and not an exception. In another instance, Christ

---

[25] Rogers, *An answer to a Book Intituled, The Lords Day proved to be the Christian Sabbath*, 4.
[26] Ibid., 15.
[27] Ibid., 17.

"traveled with Two of his Disciples that were going from Jerusalem to Immaus, which is Sixty Furlongs, which contains Seven English Miles and a Half." Christ Himself traveled on Sunday, making Rogers assert "So that it appears, that Christ had no regard to the Day, otherwise than to make it a Day of Labour."[28] In a wordier manner, Rogers explained further:

> I shall shew, that the First Commandment, that both the Angel of God and Christ himself gave forth to his Apostles, was to make the First Day of the Week (the Day of his Resurrection) a Day of Labour, by traveling out of one Province into another, as appears, Mat. 28.5 compared with the 10th and 7th Verses ... And in the 8th Verse it is said, And they departed quickly, and did run, to bring his Disciples Word. Compare this with Luke 24, 10, 11...[29]

Rogers took note that the active verbs such as "traveling," "departed," and "run" took place on the first day of the week. The amount of travel indicated on Sunday during Jesus' time could only mean that the type of Sabbath instituted by the Congregationalists was amiss.

Crisscrossing through various passages in Acts 24, 1 Corinthians 16, 2 Corinthians 8 & 9, and Romans 15, Rogers further noted that the Apostle Paul commanded work, such as the "removing of Corn," to be performed on the "first Day of the Week." This Sunday was purposefully chosen by the apostle to do "good works," and "neither *Sabbath, Lord's Day*, nor any *Assembly* asserted to be upon it." In fact, "to the contrary, [he] sheweth it to be the first Day of the Week, or beginning of a new Week, and to think of this good work upon the first Day of the week ... that this good Deed might be their first Meditation upon the beginning of a new week." Rogers made note that works, not rest, highlighted the apostles' ministry on Sundays.[30]

If the Saturday Sabbath held true as Rogers attested, then the Congregationalists were in danger of committing a twofold sin because they worked when they were supposed to rest and rested when they were supposed to work: "If this Doctrine be good, what a miserable Condition is *New-England* in, that prophanes this Fourth Commandment with

---

[28] Ibid., 9.
[29] Ibid., 8.
[30] Ibid., 11-12.

both Hands (if it stand good) in not only working upon the Day it forbids, but also *resting* from Work upon one of the Six Days, of which it saith, *Though shalt labour*."[31] This reversal of days indicated to Rogers that Congregationalists were more concerned about their manmade traditions than following Scriptural precepts. It was nothing short of vanity "to worship God by men's Traditions," and, ironically, vanity led to the very sins Congregationalists abhorred, such as idolatry and a perversion of order.[32] Rogers's writing on the Sabbath argued that discontinuing the practice was more helpful in achieving a spiritually enriched community than performing these "vain" acts of obligatory rituals every Sunday.

"Scripture Proof"

The intensity and tenacity that Rogers fused into this debate stemmed from his staunch belief in *Sola Scriptura*. He stated without reservation, "I shall enter upon this Scripture Proof about [the] First Day Sabbath, seeing the Scripture is profitable for Doctrine, for Reproof, for Correction, for Instruction." True to his word, he dutifully investigated the Bible and ventured to contextualize every passage referencing the Sabbath in its rightful historical and cultural settings. There is not a single part of Rogers's argument regarding this rite that is void of Scriptural references. Further, Rogers also took it upon himself to investigate every mention of Scripture by Wadsworth and "examine his Scripture Proof, and see what Law he produceth out of the holy Scriptures for his First Day Sabbath." After he looked through each Bible reference cited by Wadsworth, Rogers argued that his opponent did not grasp how "the word of God must be the Foundation of [the Sabbath], and the Authority of the Word the Reason of it."[33]

The irony that a sectarian would accuse a Congregationalist of deviating from the Scriptures should cause historians to pause and consider this charge. Other religious dissenters in New England, such as Anne Hutchison or Roger Williams, also used Scripture in their defense and for promoting their cause, but none were as prolific in their exposi-

---

[31] Ibid., 16.
[32] Rogers, *An Epistle to the Churches of Christ call'd Quakers*, vii.
[33] Ibid., 31.

tion of the Scriptures as Rogers. His entire defense of the Sabbath, and other Rogerene tenets, were hewn from his readings of the Bible. The amount of Scripture found in Rogers's writings perhaps should place him amongst theologians rather than religious dissenters. Page after page, citations of Scripture filled Rogers's conjectures and reasons for his stance.

Primacy of the Scriptures remained undeniably the highest priority for Rogers as he averred that "The best *interpreter* of Scripture, is Scripture, therefore I shall examine into the Place of Scripture, by other Scriptures."[34] This statement came as a response to Wadsworth's exposition of Acts 20:8. He found it problematic that Wadsworth would cite this verse in isolation, and this concern points to Rogers's methodology in incorporating several, if not many, Biblical texts in association with one another. He spent three theologically-dense pages explaining and citing many Bible passages to refute Wadsworth's teaching on this one verse. The various passages in Matthew, Luke, Acts, and 1 Corinthians each correlated to Wadsworth's exposition of Acts 20:8 and were used like chess pawns to check his opponent.

Further, the lengthy reply below provides another illustration to Rogers's primary approach to theological interpretation. Rogers contended that verses must be scrutinized and investigated in relation to others regarding the same subject. For example, when Wadsworth mentioned Genesis 2:2 to indicate that God's resting from his work should denote man's resting from theirs, Rogers replied to this one verse as follows:

> The Apostles quotes this very Place, Gen. 2.2 as is to be seen Heb. 4.4 which speaks only of God's own Rest from the Works of Creation, and we have to Account in Scripture of any Sabbath commanded or kept from Adam till Moses time; for God did not make that Covenant of the Ten Commandments till Moses time, as appears Deut. 4.13 compared with Deut. 5.2, 3 and compared with the 15th Verse, which gives the Reason of the 4th Commandment, why Israel was commanded to keep the Sabbath: For when God delivered the two Tables of the Ten Commandments, he gave Moses a particular Account about the Seventh Day Sabbath, how it was a Sign, as is to be seen, Exod. 31.12, &c. compared with the last Verse. In the 13th Verse saith the Lord, *Verily my Sabbaths ye*

---

[34] Rogers, *An answer to a Book Intituled, The Lords Day proved to be the Christian Sabbath*, 12.

shall keep, for it is a Sign between me and you. Verse 17, *It is a Sign between me and the Children of Israel.* And a Sign is not the thing signified by it, no more than the *Shadow* of a thing is the *Substance*.[35]

Clearly many in Rogers's day disagreed with his exposition of these verses, but none could deny his careful reading and use of the Holy texts. Though some charged Rogers, as he did them, of "a gross *wresting of the Scripture*, to mislead People," the primacy of Scripture in these arguments held true.[36]

For Rogers, he picked up the pen to not only justify his stance on the Sabbath but to show his opponents why their Scriptural evidence on this topic fell short. Rogers found another opportunity to do so soon in addition to his written reply to Wadsworth's *The Lord's Day*. Rogers responded to "a Pamphlet [that] is come to view" defending the Congregational Sabbath by an "Author [who] is nameless." Rogers noted that "The Title of it is, *Thesis Concerning the Sabbath*. Printed by *Timothy Green* in *New-London*" published most likely the year prior to his own publication in 1720. Rogers honed in on the the author's main "Place of Scripture ... from what is written, Mark 2:28. *Therefore the Son of Man is Lord also of the Sabbath.*" Rogers wrote that "it is needful to examine into this Place of Scripture, and see in what respect the Son of Man is to be understood the *Lord of the Sabbath*." In a long-winded manner, citing a slew of both New and Old Testament verses, Rogers concluded that "No Day of each Week, since the abolishing of the Seventh, is revealed to be the will of Christ to be kept for a Sabbath and therefore no Day to be observed as such, but to the contrary."[37]

Rogers obviously disagreed with this treatise defending the First-Day Sabbath, but his greatest contention rested in the author's perceived

---

[35] Ibid., 6.
[36] Ibid., 15.
[37] Rogers's exposition on Mark 2, Galatians 4, Colossians 2, Exodus 31, Deuteronomy 5, Ezekiel 20 reveals an in-depth examination of Sabbath principles in both the Old and New Testaments. A snippet from this portion reads: "We have here no account that Paul said to the Gentiles, come to Morrow, for to Morrow, the first Day of the Week, is the Christian Sabbath, But this Seventh Day Sabbath, which was made for Man, to be a Sign to him, as appears, Exodus 31:13, Ezekiel 20:12 compared with Deuteronomy 5:15 was abolished as appears, Colossians 2:16, 17, and not changed; for Jesus Christ God blessed for evermore, did not give Signs and Shadows under the Law to be changed, but to be fulfilled by Christ under the Gospel, by bringing in the Substance they shadowed out." Rogers, *An Answer to a Book Intituled, The Lords Day Proved to be the Christian Sabbath*, 18.

lack of Scriptural evidence. "It contains Nine Articles by way of a general Argument or Position, built upon no Foundation of Scripture, being *sophistical Sophistry*." Rogers's dual use of the root word "sophist" is an accusation against the Congregationalist author for purportedly placing human wisdom above Scriptural precepts. He contended that verses taken out of context, quoted in isolation, or wrongfully interpreted made the Congregationalists false authorities on the subject of the Sabbath. Rogers noted that apart from a rightful Scriptural interpretation, "there Is no Foundation to the Thesis, concerning the pretended Weekly Sabbath, and therefore the Thesis must fall, having no Foundation to stand upon."[38] Once again, Rogers pointed to the confused priorities that elicited laws that had a faulty biblical premise.

Like a house of cards that can fall at any moment, building a society on anything but a correct interpretation of the Scriptures seemed dangerous to Rogers. The Congregationalists' infamous belief in being their brother's keeper for covenantal reasons is well known, but what should be mentioned is Rogers's equal concern regarding God's judgment. As mentioned earlier in the chapter, Thomas Shepherd well articulated Congregational fears that God's blessings and protection upon their land would be compromised due to errant behavior or doctrine. Rogers, too, feared God's wrath like Shepherd and warned, "it is not enough that this or that Act of Worship is not forbidden in the Word of God; if it be not commanded, and you perform it, you may fear you will be found guilty, and be exposed to divine Displeasure."

Citing specific biblical example of God's fury, Rogers wrote: "Nadab and Abihu paid dear for offering in divine Worship, that which the Lord commanded them not. ... not only the *Loss of our Lives, as Nadab and Abihu did theirs, but eternal Damnation also*; as appears in your confession of Faith."[39] Throwing the Congregationalists' own words back to them, Rogers sounded the alarm of the loss of lives and eternal damnation for failing to properly understand the Scriptures. This type of dread points to Rogers's own Congregational upbringing and deeply-rooted belief in Scriptural mandates and observances. Though Rogers's interpretation regard-

---
[38] Rogers, *The Lord's Day*, 18.
[39] Ibid., 19, 22.

ing the Sabbath differed from the Congregationalists', the similarity in their commitment to a Bible-based society should not be missed.

Rogers wrote hundreds of pages on the topic of the Sabbath and perhaps the following quote best sums up his twofold contention regarding both this rite and Scriptural justifications:

> And If there be no command of god for it in the Holy Scriptures, and only your own Law in your Law Book, and your Minister's Doctrine for it, then I desire you to read and to consider what is written, Matthew 15, 7th, 8th and 9th Verses, *Ye Hypocrites ... in vain do they Worship me, searching for Doctrines the Commandments of Men.* ... Thus it appears nakedly before your Eyes, and to your Consciences, that either your Counsels, in the Confession of your Faith is very erroneous, or else your *first Day Sabbath*, if it have no command of God for it, which I can find no where throughout the whole Bible.[40]

Rogers's use of the Scriptures was double-edged in that they countered the Congregationalists' doctrinal stance while jabbing at their supposed hypocritical disposition. For Rogers, the purported glaring omission of Scriptural evidence for this rite proved that the Standing Order was an illegitimate source of authority. Thus, Rogers did not limit this type of assault to his treatises. Beyond Wadsworth and the unnamed author, Rogers also demanded answers directly from the political and religious leaders of his land.

When he was not jousting with his opponents in print, Rogers found himself also battling through the courts. Specifically addressing "Richard Christopher's Assistant, and from him to Gov. Saltonstal, and Eliphalet Adams," Rogers stated, "I request of you, as you profess yourselves to be Christians, and the Scripture to be your Rule, to give me a direct Answer to these Scriptural Questions, Romans 4:15... My question is, Hath God any Law to forbid Labour on the first Day of the Week? If he hath, quote Chapter and Verse for it, to convict us of our Error." Rogers followed up with several other questions regarding the specific name, title, and validity of the Sabbath, and he ended each question with a rendition of "If it be, pray quote the *Chapter* and *Verse*, where it is so named by God's word, if not, judge your selves."[41]

---

[40] Ibid., 21.
[41] Ibid., 19-21.

Apparently these questions were presented to "a Superior Court held in *New London*, and from them to the next General Court in that Colony, and so to the Elders and Messengers of the Churches of the Colony of Connecticut." To these courts Rogers requested "of them an Answer, upon the consideration there given." A written reply was given to Rogers, although the document no longer exists. From Rogers's words, the Congregationalists "quoted out of the Book of the confession of their own Faith." Rogers was roiled at the response that incorporated Scripture *and* the Congregational Book of Confession, which, to Rogers, was *not* on par with the Holy texts. Rogers contended that the usage of "quotations, quoted out of the Book of the Confession of their own Faith" made it clear that their convictions were not based on Scriptural precepts only but "their own pretended Faith." Further, Rogers responded by citing passages from Acts, James, Colossians, Matthew, and Hosea. He requested *another* response from these courts, but this time he asked that they "answer the said Questions by the Holy Scripture." There is no mention of a second response from the courts by Rogers or any court documents.[42]

Rogers did not hold his breath or his pen waiting for the Congregationalists to respond. He continued to write on this topic, and he also continued to put into action his thoughts on the Sabbath. He, along with his "crew," made it a point to work on Sundays, and they were fined and otherwise punished for "profaning" the Sabbath. In 1676 the fines were at five shillings apiece, but that amount increased to £5 by 1677. In addition to the monetary penalties, the Rogerenes were forced to sit in stocks and whipped for their offenses. John Rogers, a shoemaker by trade, remained undeterred by these punishments. He noted that he would have proceeded to make shoes even if his shop "stood under the window of Mr. Wetherell's house; yea, under the window of the meeting-house." While he never actually made shoes in the meetinghouse, he did try to sell them there during Sunday service in an effort to draw attention to the words he deemed had fallen on deaf Congregationalists' ears.[43]

On a spring Sunday afternoon in 1694, John Rogers burst into the meetinghouse and demanded the attention of worshipping Congregationalists in New London, Connecticut. He wheeled in a barrel full of

---

[42] Ibid., 20-21.
[43] Caulkins, *History of New London, Connecticut*, 205-206.

shoes, set them down in front of the pulpit, and started looking for buyers among the shocked and exasperated worshipers. Rogers was swiftly hauled off to prison for his flagrant demonstration of Sabbath-breaking and for purporting that "Christ drove the wheelbarrow." Rogers was fined £50 for disturbing the congregation, fined another £5 for his "evil speaking against the ordinances of God," and forced to "stand upon a ladder leaning against the gallows, with [a] rope about his neck, for a quarter of an hour" for this serious infraction against orderly worship.[44]

Incidents like these have garnered Rogerenes a reputation as a fringe sectarian group who disrupted the Standing Order through such riotous demonstrations. These actions, however, must be contextualized within the many pages authored by Rogers on theological matters. These demonstrations are only half the story told thus far. The second-half, the important theological underpinnings that moved Rogers's actions, need to be placed alongside sectarian dissent in order to create a fuller narrative of John Rogers and his followers.

Indeed, Rogerene incidents of Sabbath-breaking and disturbing Congregational worship fill the New London civil and religious annals from the Rogerene naissance in 1677 until Rogers's death in 1721. And throughout this period, civil and ecclesiastical leaders in New London considered the Rogerenes the most disruptive dissenters in their midst. By the time of this incident in 1694, Rogers was notorious for instigating such riotous demonstrations against the First Congregational Church in New London. He and his followers, the Rogerenes, waged "an open declaration of war" against "the false church" and "the beast," which represented the Congregational churches and civil authorities in Connecticut, respectively.[45] These incendiary words and unruly protests, however, were carefully constructed within Rogers's understanding of the Scriptures. His commitment to the holy texts is what allowed him to remain undeterred despite the heavy-handed reprisals and the personal loss of freedom and material wealth. Rogers's nuanced expositions of the Scriptures reveal a mind and passion that knew no other truth but what he deemed as the very words of God.

---

[44] Connecticut State Library, Superior Court Records at Hartford, May 1695.

[45] John Rogers, *A Mid-Night Cry from the Temple of God to the Ten Virgins Slumbering and Sleeping, Awake, Awake, Arise, and gird your Loyns, and trim your Lamps, for behold the Bridegroom cometh, go ye therefore out to meet him* (New London: Green, 1722), 6-7.

Chapter 3

Religious License

Individualism

There was undoubtedly much ado about the Sabbath in the "Land of Steady Habits." The strict morals guiding the inhabitants of Connecticut were manifested in a variety of forms, not the least of which centered around this weekly rite. The regularity and significance associated with the Sabbath made it a high-stakes controversy, and neither the Congregationalists nor the Rogerenes could afford to lose the argument. The Sabbath revealed the core underpinnings of their entire religious systems, and to concede on this point would unravel the bedrock upon which core theological doctrines rested.

Rogers's refusal to back down on this topic stemmed from his belief that the Bible offered liberty to believers as to when and how often they should congregate to corporately worship. From the outset, Rogers clarified that communal worship was fundamentally different from the Sabbath. Rogers maintained that the former was an observance without expiration, while the latter ended at the advent of Christ. In Rogers's view, the Congregationalists erred by fusing the two and mistakenly deeming the Sabbath a perpetual rite. To conjoin the two, Rogers declared, would be tantamount to violating man's God-given conscience by following manmade traditions in the guise of a sacrament. In his own words, Rogers argued that:

> God alone is Lord of the Conscience, and hath left it free from the Doctrines and Commandments of Men, which are in anything contrary to the Word, or not contained in it. So that to believe such Doctrines, or to obey such Commands out of Conscience, is to betray true Liberty of Conscience and Reason also ... We ought to obey God rather than Men.[1]

---

[1] John Rogers, *An Answer to a Book Intituled, The Lords Day Proved to be the Christian Sabbath*, 48.

Such biblical references pointed to a foundational Rogerene tenet: that grey areas of Scripture should never be labeled as black and white. To do so would be confusing the Scriptures and inviting idolatrous behavior. Rogers strongly believed that to convert religious license into manmade requirements was nothing short of heresy. The freedom granted within the pages of the Bible reiterated for Rogers the important doctrine of *individual* convictions regarding certain tenets. Regarding these precepts, Rogers argued that God made it clear that personal judgment should not be trampled by corporate edicts not found in the Scriptures. Rogers adamantly opposed Congregational leaders who demanded conformity in areas where Scripture had given license.

While other portions of Rogerene doctrine upheld individualism, none was as strongly apparent as in their views regarding this weekly rest. The many pages devoted to this rite pointed to Rogers's meticulous parsing of the liberties and confines of worship and rest. The prominence of the Sabbath made his interpretation all the weightier in public discourse, and Rogers hoped that other New Englanders would be persuaded that the Bible, if properly interpreted, allowed for the dismissal of the Sabbath while allowing congregants to independently choose what corporate worship entailed.

Congregationalists regarded the Rogerenes' maintenance of individualism as one of the doctrines capable of inflicting the greatest damage against the orthodoxy. One generation's virtue may well be another's vice, and individualism can certainly be viewed as such a characteristic. Individualism has become a valued American principle but was once considered to be a wayward and sinful quality in the lives of colonists. Especially for inhabitants in Congregational societies, individualism was frowned upon as a transgression against the larger community and incited suspicion from those who believed that they were their brother's keeper. While contemporary culture increasingly shies away from moral intrusion upon others, Congregationalists believed that "a concern for the morality of others was a sign of faith."[2]

Many Congregational leaders were concerned with Rogers's Sabbath beliefs, and James Fitch, Pastor of the Congregationalist

---

[2] Edmund S. Morgan, *The Puritan Family: Religion and Domestic Relations in Seventeenth-Century New England* (New York: Harper & Row), 6.

Church in Norwich, was no exception. He wrote a lengthy treatise in response to Rogers's expositions on this rite and accused Rogers of "falsely Reproach[ing]" Congregationalist laws and citing Scripture "contrary to the spiritual scope."[3] Fitch, too, claimed Scriptural passages in defending the First-Day Sabbath, but the opposing viewpoints never found common ground despite the common source. Regardless of "sound teaching," Fitch argued that Rogers refused to believe the "clear and infallible proof, that the first day of the week was called the *Lord's Day*." Fitch confessed that he had "grown[n] weary of forming his Arguments" against Rogers, since Rogers refused to listen to "sound logic." Fitch concluded that Rogers was a stubborn man and nothing remained to be done on the matter except "leave [Rogers] to his ignorance."[4]

What Congregationalists deemed ignorant, Rogers lauded as conscience. And for conscience sake, he was advocating each community's right to worship whenever it best suited them. Rogers fought for the right of each religious organization to worship on whichever day they chose and thereafter engage in as many or few somber rituals as desired. In essence, Rogers used the Sabbath to promote true congregationalism by campaigning for complete autonomy for all religious groups across New London.

As always, Rogers referred back to the Scriptures in substantiating his points. Rogers stood fast to the belief that he and his followers "may not be compelled by the Authority, to offer to God in divine Worship, that which he hath not commanded as against our Consciences." Basically, Rogers argued that edicts not found in the Scriptures were invalid. He challenged the Congregationalists "to quote to us the Place in Scripture where it is so commanded, and sen[d] it to us" if indeed God had explicitly stated that Sundays should be reserved for the Sabbath.[5] Rogers found all replies deficient of biblical proof and pressed on in his bid to annul this tenet altogether.

By abrogating the Sabbath, Rogers was in fact stating that religious groups in New London did not need to harmonize with one another on this issue of communal worship. If an entire day

---

[3] James Fitch, *An Explanation of the Solemn Advice, Recommended by the Council in Connecticut Colony, to the Inhabitants in that Jurisdiction, Respecting the Reformation of those Evils, which have been the Procuring Cause of the late Judgments upon New-England* (Boston: S. Green, 1683), 95.
[4] Ibid., 105, 108-9.
[5] Rogers, *The Lord's Day*, 21.

was dedicated to rest, it was necessary for each and every religious group to agree upon one day so that daily life would not be disrupted. Whether it was a matter of commerce, travel, or socialization, disorder would result if different groups rested on different days of the week. By absolving people of the compulsory celebration of the Sabbath, Rogers provided a way for New Londoners to worship on any day of the week without having to coordinate with one another.

The irony of Rogers's push for individualism is that he did not laud this belief as a virtue, nor did he attempt to acquire it for its own sake. Rogers was a product of his Congregationalist upbringing, and communalism was an ingrained way of life for him. To attribute individualism as Rogers's own desires would be putting the cart before the horse, so to speak. Individualism unintentionally resulted from Rogers's desire for a deeper spirituality since he was unsatisfied with the Congregationalists' interpretation of Scripture. Rogers searched the same text in hopes of creating a community that more closely resembled biblical ones, and this pursuit produced Rogerene tenets that advocated the lessening of collective worship. Once again, it was his interpretation of the Scriptures, and nothing else, that propelled Rogers's sectarian impulses.

A House of Proper Worship

Rogers's interpretation of Scripture not only undermined the Congregationalist Sabbath but also where worship should take place. He believed that the location for worship was unimportant, thereby denigrating the importance of the meetinghouse ascribed by Congregationalists. Rogers stated that the meetinghouse was no holier or more important than any other building erected because "The Worship of God is not limited to any particular Place" and a physical building could never constitute the church.[6] Rather, that title was reserved for the collective physical bodies of believers. Plainly stated, Rogers asserted that "it is the saints bodies that is the temple of God," and the place of location was not as important as those who gathered to worship.[7]

---
[6] Ibid., 2.
[7] John Rogers, *The Book of the Revelation of Jesus Christ, which God gave unto him: to show unto his servants things which were to come to pass; and Jesus Christ sent and signified it by his angles to his servant John; and now by revelation, hath opened the mystery contained in said book, unto his servant John Rogers,*

As the state-sanctioned church, Congregationalists did not have the luxury of allowing each town to choose freely the location or day for worship. Their best solution was to keep the church as the epicenter of colonial living by creating new towns when the meetinghouse became too far for residents on the outskirts to visit on a regular basis. Congregationalists trekked many miles to visit the meetinghouse for collective services, and this obligation was no mean task for those who lived far from the community hub. Physically and psychologically so situated, the meetinghouse was centrally located in each town as the center for worship. Although the meetinghouse was also used for non-religious purposes, this building symbolized a Congregationalist orderliness that held that religion must be central to personal and civic life.

The vast amount of land in the New World certainly played a significant role in these religious and political decisions. "Hiving-off" was one way that Congregationalists dealt with the expanse of land. Land was obviously a desirable commodity, since it allowed for increased industry, property, and opportunities. And land was used to offset problematic inhabitants by banishing them to distant colonies such as Rhode Island. As Sidney Mead points out, land allowed for antagonistic religious groups to be sufficiently removed from one another.[8]

Despite the variant and often positive uses of land, the abundant terrain frustrated the Congregationalists' ambition of creating close-knit communities. Dispersed inhabitants encountered difficulties in keeping one other accountable and socializing on a regular basis. Thus, the meetinghouse served as an epicenter for Congregationalists to cluster into manageable groups where inhabitants lived in relatively close proximity. Further, the meetinghouse ensured that colonists would not only settle in groups but that they would have a locale to meet regularly. Unfortunately, Congregationalists were not always able to erect meetinghouses at the pace that inhabitants settled New England, and some colonists did not have easy or any access to a meetinghouse. Rogers's call for individualized days of worship and choosing

---

of his Church and People, after a long and dark night of apostacy. The explanation being made so plain, that the eye of every spiritual reader may see how exactly things have come to pass, as were foretold by the Prophecy of this Book: and may see by it all things which are yet to come, not only to the end of this World but to the finishing of the World to come (Boston: n.p., 1720), 90-91.

[8] Sidney E. Mead, *The Lively Experiment: The Shaping of Christianity in America* (New York: Harper & Row, 1963), 13.

any location for services were potential solutions for diverse groups of religious believers spread out in distant regions. Also, individualized worship centers would ease the burdens of long-distance travel for those with back-lots in New England communities and also allow for less coordination among groups of people separated by distances. The Congregationalists, however, did not take Rogers's suggestions as creative problem-solving. The Congregationalists realized that Rogers's meetinghouse theology would result in a further individualizing of governance and accountability, and they were threatened by these prospects.

Conducting religious services apart from the meetinghouse elicited a few implications that would diminish Congregational influence. The most important consequence had to do with money. All town residents were forced to pay taxes for maintaining the meetinghouse regardless of religious persuasion, and the Congregationalists had priority in accessing the building and exclusively setting the ground rules for its usage. Rogers vehemently opposed both the taxation and stringent rules, especially after this personal experience:

> The last Fine you fined me was *Ten Shillings*. All that I did was expounding upon a Chapter in the Bible, between your Meetings, after the People were gone to Dinner, which you call a Riot. I went into no other Seat but that which I was seated in, by them whom the Town appointed to seat everyone. The building of the Meeting House cost me Three of the Best fat Cattle I had that Year, and as many shoes as was sold for *Thirty Shillings*, in Silver Money; for which said Fine of Ten Shillings, the Officer took *Ten Sheep*, as some told me that helped to drive them away.[9]

His personal experiences with the meetinghouse obviously left a bitter taste in Rogers's mouth. He was forced to pay for the creation and upkeep of the meetinghouse but was not allowed to use that space for Rogerene worship. Thus, Rogers believed that those who worshipped elsewhere should not have to pay for its upkeep, and therefore protested against compulsory taxation regarding the meetinghouse. The repeal of such a tax would mean one less hold that Congregationalists had on sectarians.

---

[9] Rogers, *The Lord's Day*, 23.

Proper Ordinances

When and where to worship occupied a large portion of Rogers's discourse with the Congregationalists and gave rise to further discussions surrounding church ordinances. Rogers's exposition on acquiring a fervent faith, this time in the realm of prayer, further augmented individualized worship which obviously concerned Congregationalists. Prayer was of utmost importance to Rogers for it was through this avenue he received salvation. Specifically, Rogers's salvation came through "Secret Prayer," in which an individual would pray to God alone in a secret place and dialogue with God silently.

Just like the Pharisees who were "zealous in [their] often Fasting and Prayers," Rogers stated that people who engaged in ritualized ordinances were so busy tending to religious deeds that they missed the heart of the message. Because people focused too much on sounding and appearing holy, they often forgot who was at the receiving end of the dialogue. Many prayers turned into performances and spectacles, and Rogers condemned "Prayer that proceeds from an unclean Heart" is an "abomination to the Lord."[10] Undeniably, Rogers argued, insincere and ostentatious displays of religiosity were indicative of "unclean hearts" because they sought the applause of men rather than communing sincerely with God. Rogers charged that false worshippers spent many hours "in the meeting house, and under a pretence of duty to God, *they made long prayers*." [11]

Rogers feared God's wrath against "this praying People" who would be scourged "with sore Destructions," for engaging in insincere acts of prayer. He believed such people pretended to dialogue with God but in actuality were conducting a performance for their church members.[12] Leaders were particularly responsible for insincere prayers because they stood "in the Synagogue, or public Assembly, and under a pretence make long prayers." Such leaders focused more on their parishioners' responses than God's. Rogers concluded "these shall receive the

---

[10] Ibid., 3.
[11] John Rogers, *John Rogers A Servant of Jesus Christ, To any of the Flock of Christ that may be scattered among the Churches of New-England, Greetings[s?]. Giving a description of the True Shepherds of Christ's Flock; and also of the Anti-Christian Ministers; According to the testimony of Jesus Christ and his Apostles, in the Holy Scriptures. As also something touching baptism and the Lord's supper* (Newport: James Franklin, 1754 [originally published 1720/1]), 25.
[12] Rogers, *An Epistle to the Churches of Christ call'd Quakers*, 81.

greater Damnation" since they draw near to god with their mouths, and honour him with their lips, but their hearts are far from him."[13] Rogers believed that the most effective types of prayers were individual, silent, and secretive. Rogers did not oppose oral prayers altogether, but he was wary of the fine line between sincerity and showmanship. As such, Rogers encouraged silent and individual prayers over external ones, even during times of communal worship. In essence, Rogers demanded that prayer should be without fanfare and without the approval of any other.

One way to encourage private prayer was the leniency of prayer time. No established prayer agendas were strictly enforced within Rogerene worship because such "set Times of Prayer" were conducive to hypocrisy. Tantamount to worshiping "God in Forms," Rogerenes considered that such ritualized prayers often sought the approbation of men rather than God. Further, Rogerene prayers focused on the necessity of waiting upon God for an answer. Rogers contended that oral prayers made the supposed dialogue into more of a monologue but silent prayers allowed for silent meditation until "it pleased God to answer his request."[14] Just as in didactic communication where pauses indicate contemplation or a thoughtful response, Rogers believed in giving God time to answer prayers. Reflective silences varied in length, which served as another rationale for dispensing with scheduled prayer. God could easily call a person into conversation outside of prescribed prayer times, and the Almighty's responses may linger without a definite timeframe for quite some time.

Rogers desired that each believer have a vital relationship with God, which could be signified though a dynamic prayer life. A two-way dialogue with God was indispensable in obtaining a sincere faith because the absence of it meant the loss of true communication with the Almighty. Rogers stressed that "Prayer is of no use without a Conversation answerable thereunto," and without such exchanges, one-sided, grandiose prayers were an "Abomination to the Lord." He warned that God visited people who engaged in such prayers with "sore Destruction."[15]

Just as it was important for God to answer man's request, Rogers taught that man's reciprocation to God's voice was absolutely vital.

---

[13] Rogers, *A Mid-Night Cy from the Temple of God*, 96.
[14] Ibid., 3.
[15] Rogers, *An Epistle to the Churches of Christ Call'd Quakers*, 80-81.

God's voice mostly pointed believers back to Scripture, which Rogers believed spoke clearly into the hearts and minds of true followers. Quoting from Isaiah 10:5 and 33:14, Rogers reminded his followers of God's warning to "Obey my Voice" and "walk ye in all the ways that I have commanded you, that it may be well unto you."[16] The many Bible passages that Rogers cited regarding various tenets, including the Sabbath, revealed to him God's "voice" on these matters. For Rogers, what was gleaned through intimate prayers with God always correlated with the Scriptures. It was man's response, then, to answer God by obeying the commands as prescribed in these holy texts.

The Congregational Sabbath that included "many prayers in public assemblies" served as proof to Rogers that the Standing Order did not understand the Scriptures accurately. Rogers condemned their times of public prayer as nothing more than outward displays of religiosity and stated that they were in the "same manner as the false church of old" by "attending [to their] pretended gospel ordinances." Their "fair pretences of worshipping God" were "guilded outwardly." Using stronger language, Rogers stated that people who engaged in such prayer were like "decked harlots" arrayed in "purple and scarlet colour," who "allure[d] her lovers" through much outward parading.[17]

Rogers viewed various forms of religious pomp as sure evidence for haughtiness that God would condemn, and he cited the wigs and robes worn by Congregationalist ministers as colonial renditions for outward guilding and scarlet array. The following event reveals the turbulent relationship that the Rogerenes had with the Puritan elites that resulted from divergent opinions on such theological matters. In particular, Gurdon Saltonstall had a historically acrimonious relationship with Rogers. He served as the minister of the Congregational church in New London from 1691 until he became governor of Connecticut in 1708.

Rogers would often use Saltonstall as a prime and glaring example of religious ostentation and self-glorification. One example is Rogers's publication, *An Impartial Relation of an Open and Publick Dispute Agreed upon Between Gurdon Saltonstall*, published in 1701. Unfortunately no extant copies exist, but the title suggests that

---

[16] Ibid., 80-84.
[17] Rogers, *The Book of the Revelation of Jesus Christ*, 176.

Rogers levied complaints against the Puritan leader and pulled no punches.[18] The primary sources that do exist and shed light on the contention between the two are transcripts of court documents and church records. These sources indicate that their quarrel was personal as well as doctrinal. A few incidents between the two preceded this publication and affected Rogers's feelings toward Saltonstall.

A special incident in Rogers's life in 1691 known as the "wig" episode started the Rogers-Saltonstall feud. As a protest against the full-bottomed wigs worn by some Congregational clergymen, Rogers put a wig in the offering box situated next to the pulpit as a joke. Rogers was inspired to send such a gift to coincide with Saltonstall's ordination as the pastor of the First Congregational Church in New London on November 1691. On January 22, 1692, just one month after Saltonstall's ordination, Rogers sent his "gift" on the special day dedicated to the "Contribution to the Ministry." The Congregationalists obviously did not share Rogers's sense of humor since they demanded reprisal. Before the authorities forced Rogers to repent, he willingly apologized for the matter in person and by issuing a written apology for his "rash behavior" of "unadvisedly sending a perewigg." He asked "all those whom [he] had offended" to accept his "publique acknowledgement as full satisfaction."[19]

The hostility continued in 1698 when Saltonstall sued Rogers for defamation for causing a "great scandal" by publicly insulting him. At the New London County Court on September 20, 1698, Saltonstall addressed members of the court, Captain Daniel Wetherell and Justices William Ely and Nathaniel Lynde, and recounted how Rogers alleged that he had promised to hold a public dispute on the holy Scriptures but reneged and was therefore not a man of his word. The court found in favor of Saltonstall and condemned Rogers for "rais[ing] a lying, false and scandalous report against" him. Rogers was forced to pay the costs of court, £1, 10 shilling, and was also fined £600 for the offence.[20] An officer of the court confiscated ten of Rog-

---

[18] John Rogers, *An Impartial Relation of an Open and Publick Dispute Agreed upon Between Gurdon Saltonstall, Minister of the Town of New-London, and John Rogers of the Same Place* (Philadelphia: Reynier Jansen, 1701).
[19] Connecticut State Library, New London Country Records, Vol. 4, Folder 46.
[20] Caulkins, *History of New London, Connecticut*, 213. Monetary citation from Bolles and Williams, *The Rogerenes*, 29.

ers's sheep as payment for court charges and returned a second time to take a cow for additional payment, stating that the ten sheep were insufficient to cover all costs. The payment of £600 was not recorded but there is evidence that the Rogers faced financial difficulty in 1698.[21]

Despite these penalties, Rogers remained undeterred. The amount of writing that Rogers dedicated to theologies leading to individualism connotes the importance he placed on these topics. Matters concerning the Sabbath, meetinghouse, and prayer were especially significant in that they touched daily, if not weekly, colonial living. Rogers did not intend to interpret Scripture to advocate for the fragmentation of communal living. However, that was the result. Individualism that resulted from Rogerene theology meant less communal activity, which would lead to a more pluralistic society.

The Rogerenes' views on topics that promoted individualism obviously threatened Congregationalists, but other divergent doctrinal points did not cause much friction between the two groups since these doctrines were not seen as much of a threat. For example, regarding the sacraments, Rogerenes condemned the orthodoxy for failing to follow Scriptural precepts and naturally defended his own expositions. However, Rogers's view on the sacraments did not result in individualized living. Rogers's only contention on matters of baptism was that the Congregationalists were satisfied with "ha[ving] a bason of water brought into their meeting-house," when the Bible illustrated "all baptisms to be" in areas where "there was much water." Rogers emphasized how Congregationalists conducted sprinkle baptism when "the scripture of the apostles teacheth them otherwise."[22]

Much like his condemnation of the inexact imitations of biblical baptism, Rogers also condemned Congregationalists for inappropriately conducting communion. The two main points of contention focused on the time of day communion was administered and the food items used in this rite. Rogers adamantly adhered to holding communion in the evening and serving meat as part of the sacrament.[23] Rogers found it peculiar that Congregational communion contained only the eating of bread and drinking of wine when clearly Jesus and his disciples

[21] Bolles and Williams, *The Rogerenes*, 195.
[22] Ibid., 13.
[23] Ibid., 89-97.

"did not only eat Bread, but eat their Bread, with their other meat."[24] Preferably lamb was the chosen meat for Rogerene communion meals since it pointed to the "figure of Christ, the real Lamb of God, who was betrayed the same night in which [communion] was offered."[25]

Once again Rogers went back to the Scriptures to validate his point: "But as to the Lord's Supper, it was always attended at Supper-time: It was *first instituted by Christ at Supper*, as appears, Matthew 26:20." Further, Rogers stated that the Apostle Paul reiterated the teachings of Christ as stated in "1 Corinthians 11:23 compared with the 25th Verse, *For I have received of the Lord that which I delivered on to you, that the Lord Jesus, the same Night in which he was betrayed took Bread, etc. After the same manner, also he took the Cup, when they had supped etc."*[26] The Rogerenes remained committed to their version of the Lord's Supper, and no substantial correction by the Congregationalists are recorded regarding these doctrines.[27]

It appears that the sacraments took a backseat to other theological points that attempted to undercut Congregational order. No legal punishments are recorded of the Rogerenes practicing communion in their own way. While Congregationalists found Rogers's contention on this point troublesome, it was not an imminent threat to the well-being of their community. As such, Congregational leaders did not expend energy in trying to uproot this practice. Likewise, Rogerenes were allowed to baptize their members in a body of water so long as they did not do it on the Congregational Sabbath. The orthodoxy seemingly triaged their battles against the Rogerenes, and so prioritized their attention on matters that most threatened their grip on society.

The Courts

For Rogers, he saw no discrepancy in the importance of these doctrines since they were equally mandated by Scripture. Refusing to back down on any of these points, Rogers fought for his religious

---
[24] Rogers, *A Mid-Night Cry from the Temple of God*, 89-97.
[25] Rogers, *John Rogers A Servant of Jesus Christ*, 16.
[26] Rogers, *The Lord's Day*, 13-14.
[27] An important study to consider when looking at sectarianism and the sacraments is E. Brooks Holifield, *The Covenant Sealed: The Development of Puritan Sacramental Theology in Old and New England, 1570-1720* (New Haven: Yale University Press, 1974).

rights by exhausting every opportunity available. Ultimately, his variant theological beliefs brought him before many colonial courts. Rogers argued that every English citizen was afforded the "Extraordinary privilidg" of religious freedom after the reign of Charles II, and this freedom should rightfully be extended to all sectarians.[28] He aptly utilized local courts in matters of religion after he had failed to receive an adequate reply from religious leaders within the Congregational fold. Of course what constituted a sufficient reply was Rogers's opinion. In one instance, Rogers had studied the Congregationalists document entitled "Confessions of their own Faith," and he was curious as to some portions of their theology. He approached the ministers about these questions, only to be "turned out" without answer. Rogers, then, took his questions to the local court, believing that the civil authorities must know the doctrines that they were supporting. The court dismissed Rogers's questions, and, instead, condemned him for "taking it upon himself" to "usurp the power to judge, both our Governour and our Laws." They charged him for his "bold rebuke" and "gross appearance of irreverence" toward the judge.[29]

Not to be deterred, Rogers approached the New London Superior Court, only to be quickly dismissed. Then, Rogers approached the General Court of Connecticut on grounds of appeal. The General Court carefully reviewed Rogers's complaints that Congregational parishioners were being abused since they were being forced to pay more than their minister's salary. The forced payment of pastoral wages incited rage in Rogers, but to add insult to injury, he believed that the New London parish demanded additional payments for special occasions, such as baptisms and ordinations. Ultimately, Rogers "could obtain no Answer but Persecution," and all three courts rejected his charges. Still, Rogers continued to use the legal route to demonstrate against Congregational practices.[30]

Despite the lack of response, Rogers continued to access the courts in order to rectify what he deemed were breaches in Congregational church action and ordinances. Often Rogers failed to find any sympathizers in colonial courts and threatened to take his case to England. On occasion his warnings turned into reality but mostly

---

[28] Connecticut State Library, Ecclesiastical Affairs, I:132.
[29] James Fitch, An *Explanation of the Solemn Advice, Recommended by the Council in Connecticut Colony* (Boston: Green, 1683), location 1079 of 1183.
[30] Rogers, An Answer to a Book Intituled, The Lords Day Proved to be the Christian Sabbath, 18-19.

Rogerene legal matters remained a New-World affair. Although the Crown was rarely petitioned, the many insinuations by Rogers to involve the Mother Country brought him a measure of power. In each threat to appeal to English courts, Rogers reminded New London leaders that Connecticut's charter was tenuous, knowing that the colonial courts would take great measures to side-step scrutiny by the Crown.

The following example shows how Rogerene threats to involve the Crown were used to their advantage. The event started when a charge against Rogers of some significance was brought forward in 1711. Although the details are unknown, it appears Rogers was charged for a serious crime supposedly committed in Long Island along with John Jackson, an alleged co-conspirator of African descent. Rogers testified that Congregationalists had wrongfully attempted to place him in Long Island at the time of the crime, when in actuality he resided "within the Government of New York."[31]

Rogers took this case to a higher court, where, instead of being greeted with a jury trial, he was fined twenty shillings by the Superior Court. When Rogers refused to pay the fine, land was taken from him as payment. Rogers explained that this land was purchased for his son, John Rogers, Jr., with his son's own money. After the land was taken, Rogers, Jr. repurchased his initial plot of land and was given a patent. Rogers made an unveiled threat that if this land were to be confiscated again, he would take his case to England. He referred to patents issued by the Mother Country as he stated to the New London County court "you gave him a Patent for it, I think as substantial as your Patent from the Crown of England for your Government upon all Accounts, being sealed with your Seal, and with your present Governours Hand, and your Secretarys to it." There is no further citation of this land being taken from Rogers.[32]

John Rogers greatly resented the fact that the Congregationalists, who in England had been relegated as "Protestant Dissenters," were thrusting their beliefs upon everyone in New England. He found this to be in violation of "the Immutable Laws of God and Nature," which provided every person the right to worship according to "Liberty of Conscience." Rogers used the courts to remind Congregation-

---
[31] Ibid., 25.
[32] Ibid.

alists of this fact. One such instance occurred in 1695 after Sabbath demonstrations brought the Rogerenes a series of reprisals once again. After being heavily fined for a number of such infractions, John Rogers and Richard Steere petitioned the Court of Assistants to overturn these charges. In this petition, Rogers and Steere argued that New London civil authorities had no right to intervene in church affairs and accused the Congregationalists of having "vaulted themselves" unlawfully "into the Saddle of the National Church." Using the term "national church" reminded the Congregationalists that the true sanctioned church of the Mother Country was the Anglican denomination.[33]

Rogers did not state that all existing state-supported religions were false or should be stripped of their authority over the citizenry. In fact, Rogerene doctrine advocated the state support of legitimate religious systems. Although Rogers diverged with Congregationalists on doctrinal matters, these differences were not the main cause for concern. If that were the case, then any religion save the Rogerenes would be an illegitimate choice for state support according to Rogers.[34]

Compatible religious tenets with Rogerene views did not validate state-supported status. More importantly, Rogers contended that the church upheld by the state should remit equitable practices to its local inhabitants. Fleecing the parishioners with excessive taxes and confiscating lands and goods for nonattendance were causes for dismissal. And Rogers made it clear that Congregationalists were engaging in these unjust practices and therefore should be censured from receiving state support. On the other hand, Rogers amicably accepted Anglicanism as the English choice for state support although their doctrines were quite dissimilar. Perhaps a two-fold reason for their agreement might be because the English Crown made it easier for religious dissenters to freely worship while Anglicanism was not a dominating presence in New England.

Rogers's repeated run-ins with the law might indicate that he had little regard for regulations but his writings indicate otherwise. Rogers was compliant towards all civic laws so long as they did not violate his religious convictions. Despite his difficulties with the colonial legal system, he still had faith and respect for the courts when

---

[33] Connecticut State Library, Ecclesiastical Affairs, I:132-34.
[34] Ibid., 132.

it came to nonreligious matters. He often used the courts for personal reasons and sought the advice of magistrates to quell domestic issues. The Rogerenes as a whole were litigious people who were embroiled in a host of personal matters. Moreover, the Rogerses fought one another legally in matters beyond inheritance and often found themselves in legal disputes with their neighbors. In 1705, James Rogers, Jr. brought a lawsuit against Sarah Rogers for threatening him with a pitchfork. And John Rogers, Jr. and Mary Rogers were recorded as having physically assaulted one another a few times in that same year. Besides these familial disputes, Rogerenes were entangled in a host of other legal matters.[35]

A Move Towards Toleration

The Rogerenes hoped that the state would recognize their views on the Sabbath, the meetinghouse, and other civic and religious rights they found to be God-given. Their commitment to religious freedom interpreted in the Scriptures inspired the Rogerenes to fight hard and make their voices heard. Unfortunately for these sectarians, their complete disavowal of the Sabbath and their push to worship at diverse locations were never embraced in colonial times. The state, however, did make concessions in the form of toleration laws. The Toleration Acts of 1689 and 1708, the repeal of "Quaker laws" in 1702, and tax exemptions for dissenters instituted between 1727 and 1729 are good indicators of the dissenters' gains. The 1708 Toleration Act in particular gave hope to dissenters regarding the Sabbath because this law, modeled after the 1689 English Toleration Act, allowed for the separate worship of "sober dissenters." So long as dissenters proved to be members of a religious institution sanctioned by the state, they were allowed to hold devotions separately from Congregational churches.

Much like the inadvertent push for individualism through an exacting reading of Scripture, toleration laws were the unintended outcome of pushing to make sectarian doctrine a legitimate part of religious society. Rogerenes fought hard to make their doctrinal expositions a reality in colonial lives and the results were the increase in toleration laws. These toleration laws, however, were never the prin-

---
[35] Connecticut State Library, Court Papers, Volume 9.

cipal aim of the Rogerenes. Not all sectarians viewed toleration acts as steps leading to a place without state-directed worship. There were religious dissenters, such as the Rogerenes, who pushed for these laws in their bid to address immediate needs, such as the right to proselytize, assemble, and forgo compulsory tithing. And sectarians did not always view toleration laws as precursors to religious plurality. The Rogerenes never lobbied to dismantle the union between church and state, and their treatises are clear indicators that these sectarians supported a state-sanctioned church within proper biblical confines.

Rogers never advocated the separation of church and state because these entities were intricately linked in his mind. While he acknowledged their disparate roles in society, he did not compartmentalize civic affairs from religious ordinances. Rather, he viewed all facets of life as part-and-parcel of God's making in which the Almighty should reign unhindered. Rogers fought unremittingly against religious laws that impeded sectarian worship because his ultimate objective was to adhere to Scriptural mandates in every segment of society.

The church and state were separated in Rogers's mind only in that they were different branches of power. When Rogers stated "But Church and state we know have allwayes been accounted two different things," he was not referring to their divorce but how these entities should be properly related. Rogers meant that "the terms Presbiterian Church and the Terms Conecticut Government" cannot "be sinonimous" any more than "the Church of England may be called the Regal Government of England." The church should supervise the spiritual aspects of society while the state managed civic affairs, but the two should work in tandem to create a stable and prosperous nation. The state owed it to its citizenry, according to Rogers, to uphold the *true* church.[36]

The state had the responsibility of supporting correct doctrine but needed to recognize civic limitations. Rogers argued that the "Liberty of Conscience is every mans natural birthright" and is an "undeniable Principle" of truth found in the Holy Texts. This meant that men should not be forced to subscribe to a religion they did not sincerely accept, nor be obliged to forgo civil rights or property due to religious

---

[36] Connecticut State Library, Ecclesiastical Affairs, I:134.

reasons. Individual convictions, for Rogers, trumped any church or state mandate since he believed he was answering to the highest call of all.[37]

---

[37] Ibid., 132.

Chapter 4

Doctrines of Man and the Role of the Spirit

Religious Landscape

The New World was a vast and sparsely populated place in the seventeenth century, and colonists flocked together into settlements, hoping to create areas insulated from the dangerous wilderness. Each town's fortification had a dual purpose of banning physical as well as ideological threats since communities often consisted of people with similar convictions. Dominant political and religious principles guided each enclave's day-to-day affairs and served as moral pillars that upheld the inhabitants' integrity. Congregational tenets ruled in New England, Anglican beliefs dominated in the middle and southern colonies, and Quakerism prevailed in Pennsylvania. But there were always dissenting views in the midst of the governing forces, and some ideals divergent from the ruling majority managed to survive while others eventually disbanded.

Religious sensibilities and authority were in flux in colonial America during the second-half of the seventeenth century. Vacant pulpits, scattered congregations, and a lack of religious cohesion plagued almost every colony outside of and some within New England. The Puritan stronghold often buffered this region from such unrest, but they had problems of their own. The rise of sectarian presence within Congregational societies attests to this fact. Offshoots from established dissenting traditions further demonstrate that the splintering of religious ideas had the potential to proliferate. The creation of a marginalized sect such as the Rogerenes proves that even the Congregational elites could not always successfully dictate religious order to their citizenry.

The failure of the Rogerenes to create a more vibrant and lasting denomination points to their doctrine rather than the religious milieu of their time. The gaps in leadership in colonial New London and the Congregationalists' failure to implement uniformity gave ample opportunity for the Rogerenes to establish themselves. The Rogerenes fought to take root in Congregational New London but failed to create an enduring denomination. They introduced themselves with great fanfare in 1677 but had largely disbanded by the American Revolution and eventually disappeared by the early nineteenth century. The inability of the Rogerenes to flourish beyond a 200-member sect and exist for a longer period of time can be traced back to the core doctrine established during John Rogers's tenure as the sect's leader. Rogerene theology was a complex mix of variant theologies that only appealed to a small minority of people. Rogers was undoubtedly committed to the primacy of the Scriptures, but his unique and careful exegesis of both the Old and New Testaments did not persuade the masses.

Rogerene doctrine failed to resonate with many colonists since New World settlers were looking for security in an oft-changing continent. Many settlers longed to be just that – settled – both physically and mentally since the encroachments of Native American enemies, rampant diseases, and unpredictable weather continually threatened at bay. Religion undoubtedly brought many settlers a measure of reassurance and hope when forces beyond their control loomed large. A fledgling sect with fluid tenets surely could not provide these colonists with the degree of assurance that they craved and needed.

Also, unlike many dissenting New England sects, the Rogerenes did not have Old World counterparts who could lend them a measure of credibility or assistance. In the late seventeenth-century, the Quakers, Baptists, and Sabbatarians were still largely extensions of their English brethren and relied heavily upon their home countrymen for direction and leadership. As the first indigenous sect in the colonies, the Rogerenes did not have such luxuries and relied on their own resources to forge a religious community. John Rogers's leadership skills and the Rogerses' wealth and affluence were the main backing behind this movement, and both seemed paltry in comparison to religious establishments rooted in the Mother Country.

The lack of Old World support or the fluctuation in their theology, however, was not the central cause for the eventual Rogerene dismantlement. The core issue stemmed from the solidified portions of their doctrines that failed to provide distinct alternatives to Congregational tenets. While Rogerene actions, such as their rancorous demonstrations, appeared too radical, their theology emerged as rather tepid when juxtaposed to sectarian thought. In matters of salvation, for example, the Rogerenes, like Congregationalists, believed in predestination, thereby alienating those who believed that their own industry or good behavior could facilitate entry to heaven.

Established churches, by definition, needed to compromise their original principles in order to invite and cater to the entire community, which fell under its jurisdiction. The Congregationalists did just that when they passed the Halfway Covenant in 1662. Sectarians, on the other hand, needed to create a viable alternative to the state-sanctioned church, which often meant that dissenting ideals had to be markedly different compared to the prevailing ideology. The Rogerenes demanded radical action from their followers but failed to provide a radical theology that justified their insurgency. Rogerene doctrine that dealt with salvation, education, and the importance of Scripture contained too many overlapping elements with the ruling Congregationalists to present a distinct path to understanding the Almighty.

Despite the similarities between Rogerene and Congregational tenets, no one accused John Rogers of being orthodox. Just as there were intersecting doctrines between these two groups, there were also differences in their outlook regarding many tenets such as the Sabbath, baptism, and prayer. Congregationalists were rigorous theologians who did not take lightly even the slightest deviation from their beliefs. But on matters of salvation, Rogerenes were too moderate in theology to be cast among the radical sectarians, such as the Quakers and Sabbatarians, and too militant in action to be categorized among the respectable dissenters, such as the Baptists and Anglicans. The Rogerenes found themselves in a theological no-man's-land and teetered on a doctrinal fence that appealed to very few New Londoners.

The Way to Salvation

Rogerene doctrine on salvation is surprisingly traditional and somewhat in line with Reformation principles. Rogers held partially to Calvinistic notions of predestination and stated "God chose us, before the Foundation of the World, that we should be holy with his own holiness." Therefore, Rogers argued, God chose a select group of people for salvation, but this group was not necessarily identified through one type of religion, sect, or following. Just as Rogers received salvation as a Sabbatarian, he believed there were saved souls outside of the Rogerene fellowship and perhaps even some within the Congregational fold. Salvation was facilitated "through free Grace in Christ," he believed, rather than through certain principles or laws. People could never achieve salvation by works or choosing the right fellowship, but, instead, salvation was the gift of grace by God through Jesus Christ.[1]

On a basic level, Rogers's theology leveled the proverbial playing field in that any man or woman might be saved. Logically the principle of choice contained a downside, where if God chose some for salvation, he also chose others for eternal damnation. Rogers, however, disagreed with such a rationale and stated that "for God never foreordained any man to Damnation, but his Judgment is just, for his transgressing of the Law, and God's call to undone Sinners, is by his own Spirit." Here, Rogers stated that God never willed any person to hell but such a person was so sentenced due to his own sins against God's laws. God did not choose some for damnation but, rather, rescued some for salvation. Rogers believed that after the fall of Adam, all of mankind was destined for hell and justly so due to their sins. Rogers reasoned that God in his mercy chose some to spend eternity with him through the grace of Christ. Rogers did not explain why God chooses some and not others, although he believed that God's judgment was just.[2]

While a large portion of Rogerene doctrine on salvation centered

---

[1] John Rogers, *A Mid-Night Cry from the Temple of God to the Ten Virgins Slumbering and Sleeping, Awake, Awake, Arise, and gird your Loyns, and trim your Lamps, for behold the Bridegroom cometh, go ye therefore out to meet him* (New London: Green, 1722), 44.
[2] Ibid., 45.

on predestination, it also involved elements of Quaker principles. The mix of two seemingly opposing theologies was difficult for many New Londoners to accept, thereby truncating the level of appeal the Rogerenes had on their local inhabitants. Although Rogers did not accept universality of salvation as a legitimate doctrine, he believed that the inner light within each person played a vital part in salvation. Central to Rogers's dispute with the Quakers was the issue of this light within, a topic that Rogers extensively researched and expounded upon. Rogers agreed with the Quakers that there was an inner consciousness or voice given to all men, but he disagreed that this light produced salvation. Opposing the universality of salvation theory, Rogers said this inner light was the light that led one to the *possibility* of salvation, not to salvation itself. Rogers purported that this light within is given to men "not because he hath been obedient to the Light, but to enable him to be obedient to the Light within." Rogers believed that every man had the potential for salvation but surety of salvation could never be secured through an inner light. The inner light was reliant upon the movement of the "Spirit of Truth," which was given at the impulse of God's choice. Ultimately, whether that inner light would manifest into salvation was up to God's discretion.[3]

Rogers believed that God's reasoning for salvation was unknowable, but he confirmed the predictable steps that accompanied salvation. The first step was the conviction of sin, which Rogers called either the "Ministration of the Law" or "Light of Condemnation"; the second step was the regeneration of new life, which he called the "Ministration of the Gospel of Jesus Christ" or the "Light of our Justification." The first state readied one for salvation, while the second confirmed it; and both phases came from "one and the self-same God." If the first step was a jumping stone to salvation and the second a substantiation of it, then it seems logical to assume that salvation was actually acquired somewhere in between these two steps.[4]

In order to understand this "midway" salvation, Rogers more fully expounded upon the endpoints. The Light of Condemnation shone in the hearts of unbelievers and revealed the knowledge of sin. Rogers

---
[3] Ibid., 44-46.
[4] Ibid., 44-45.

believed that the Ministration of the Law did not expose specific sins, such as adultery or stealing, because it was the sinful *nature* of mankind rather than the specific manifestations of sin that was revealed to the repentant heart. The sinner accepted the knowledge of man's depravity in comparison with God's holiness and understood that no good act could counter his sinful disposition.

Knowledge of one's sinful nature, however, was insufficient to facilitate salvation because knowledge does not necessarily lead to obedience. Rogers tried to explain this point by using Adam and Eve's experience in the Garden of Eden as an illustration. Upon eating the fruit from the tree of knowledge, Adam and Eve's awareness of sin grew but their obedience did not. Adam vainly tried to "cover his shame or nakedness by his own wisdom and works." Instead of exhibiting remorse or compliant hearts, Adam and Eve's newfound knowledge only precipitated further strife between themselves and with God.[5]

Rogers said that it was not any knowledge that saved a man, but faith-producing knowledge that allowed the acceptance of what Jesus did on the cross of Calvary. That is, it is by faith that a man was able to arrive at the ministration of the Gospel of Jesus Christ. Because the Ministration of the Law revealed man's sinful nature, the repentant heart understood that "there is none righteous in himself, no, not one." Rogers stated that the knowledge of sin drove a man to look for a Savior, who alone could justify sin through the atonement of a blood sacrifice. Once the acceptance of "his Justification thro' Faith in the Blood of Jesus Christ" became a reality, the sinner was now saved through faith. It was the belief that saved a man and allowed "the free Pardon of God" to enter into a man's heart and "escape the Justice of God's Wrath" which was "justly due to them" as with all mankind. The point of salvation between the two-step ministrations outlined by Rogers was none other than the point of faith.[6]

Just as Luther proclaimed *sola fide*, Rogers agreed that faith alone could save man from eternal judgment. Faith, however, was not a blank check leading to salvation, but the *type* of faith was also a deter-

---
[5] John Rogers, *An Epistle to the Churches of Christ call'd Quakers; And another epistle to the Seventh Day Baptists, with several Theological Essays* (New York: William Bradford, 1705), 16-17, 19-20, 36.
[6] Ibid., 19-20, 36.

mining factor. Rogers distinguished dead faith from living faith, stating that a dead faith "never come[s] to Repentance" and refuses "to break off from their sins, and so never come[s] to partake of that mercy of God by Jesus Christ." Those with a dead faith "idolize God's ordinances," thereby relying on works and self-aggrandizing practices, such as long public prayers. The penalty for a dead faith is equal to that for the unsaved, and Rogers said "they shall receive their portion with hypocrites, even in the hottest place of hell fire, where they shall ever be Tormented, not only for their actual sins, in transgressing the law of God, but chiefly for their hypocrisie."[7]

Contrary to false faith, true faith provided the new believer with supernatural sight, which Rogers continually referred to throughout his writings. He stated that true faith "gives a sight of what the ear before did only hear" and allowed the eye to "seeth the truth of what the Scriptures before made report of." This type of faith confirmed for Rogerenes that "their faith is not upon a bare report, but from the sight of their own eyes." Rogers believed a living faith enabled human eyes to see into the Scriptures in a literal sense, although he never explicitly stated what the eye beheld.[8] Presenting a complex theology that New Londoners deemed neither here nor there caused the Rogerenes to lose credibility as sectarians. Quakers and Sabbatarians suggested that Rogerene theology reeked of Congregational influence and relied too heavily on Reformation principles.

The fee for participating in a sectarian cause in New England was indeed costly, and there needed to be a justifiable reason to join such a risky venture. Dissenters faced the certainty of fines, whipping, public humiliation, and physical incarceration, and only a worthy cause could offset these difficulties. The Rogerenes appeared to ask their members to pay an exorbitant price by engaging in boisterous demonstrations, but they did not provide adequate theological compensation. The Rogerenes fell short in presenting their theology as a distinct alternative to Congregationalism.

Of those opposing Congregational theology, Sabbatarians and Quakers were the most concerned that Rogers relied too heavily on or-

---
[7] Rogers, *A Mid-Night Cry from the Temple of God*, 93-94, 101.
[8] Ibid., 93-94, 100-3.

thodox views. Ironically, Rogers had the most contact with European Quakers and Sabbatarians, and he derived a good portion of Rogerene doctrine from these sects. Many of the sectarian ideals that Rogers adopted were considered Old World beliefs, although Rogers himself never traveled to England or Ireland. Instead, sectarians brought Old World ideals to Rogers, who pondered their legitimacy and place in his sect.

Traveling Quakers did their best to dissuade New Londoners from agreeing with Congregational laws, and John Rogers often found himself in the company of such itinerant Friends. William Edmundson, an Irish Quaker, made his second trip to the New World in 1675 and spent a considerable amount of time with Rogers in Hartford before returning home. Rogers listened to Edmundson's lectures for hours at a time and then returned the favor by positing his own views on doctrinal matters. Edmundson followed Rogers to New London where he made the acquaintance of other Rogerenes, whom he found "loving and tender."[9]

Samuel Bownas, a traveling English Quaker, also made a theological impression upon John Rogers. In 1703, Bownas was visiting the New World but was temporarily imprisoned in Hampstead, Long Island. Rogers visited Bownas for many days traveling "near two hundred miles on purpose to visit [him]," and the two discussed a host of issues. Among the topics were women taking part in church meetings, believers being empowered by the Spirit of God, the questionable legitimacy of water baptism, and, of course, the way to salvation.[10]

Traveling sectarians obviously transported Old World ideals but so did religious dissenters who were settled in New England in the seventeenth century. Although the Quakers and Sabbatarians had already been established in the colonies by the time of the Rogerenes' rise, these sectarian doctrines were largely based upon European persuasion. By 1674, when the Rogerenes were founded, the Quakers had been established in the colonies since 1657 and the Sabbatarians since 1671. They were still principally extensions of their English counterparts and relied

---

[9] John R. Bolles and Anna B. Williams, *The Rogerenes: Some Hitherto Unpublished Annals Belonging to the Colonial History of Connecticut* (Boston: Stanhope Press), 134.
[10] Samuel Bownas, *The Life, Travels, and Christian Experiences of Samuel Bownas* (Linfield: The Schools of Industry, 1836), 110, 118.

heavily upon their home countrymen for direction and leadership.

For example, when John Rogers joined their ranks in 1674, the English Sabbatarians still influenced the Newport Sabbatarians through written exchanges. Several extant letters show that Newport Sabbatarians wrote to the Bell Lane Church in England for advice. On March 6, 1670 Edward Stennet, a Sabbatarian in England, replied to the Newport Sabbatarians' query about those who formerly accepted and then denounced Sabbatarian principles. Stennet advised them to "withdraw yourselves, and not be partakers of other men's sins" and anyone who holds "communion with those apostates from the truth" ought to be "fairly dismissed from the church."[11] Staying true to Stennet's advice for many years, the Newport Sabbatarians did indeed exile impenitent members, among them John Rogers in 1677.

Before the eighteenth century, the Quakers in the New World were financially, theologically and customarily an extension of their brethren in the Old World. Rogers's exchange with visiting Friends from Europe or those from nearby colonies proved to be theologically one in the same, and his encounters with neighboring or English and Irish Quakers reflected similar exchanges. New England Quakers were principally managed by leaders in England; and as Jonathan Chu points out, by 1672 George Fox was in firm control in England and "had begun to extend to New England the structure of monthly and yearly meetings for business that gave the sect a more structured, disciplined, and centralized denominational cast."[12] The teachings and overall religious culture of Old and New World Quakers were very similar before the eighteenth century.

No matter how much Rogers desired to embrace sectarian principles however, he was trapped in a Congregational mindset that he could not escape. Although New London was the most open to outside influences among all Connecticut settlements, Congregationalism was still the dominant theology and had seeped into Rogers's foundational understanding of God. Rogerene theology, laden with mainstream Congregational beliefs, is a testament to this fact. Rogers was undoubtedly fascinated with sectarian beliefs, but he translated these principles

---

[11] Isaac Backus, *A History of New-England With Particular Reference to the Denomination of Christians Called Baptists* (Newton: The Backus Historical Society, 1871), 2:501.
[12] Jonathan M. Chu, *Neighbors, Friends, or Madmen: The Puritan Adjustment to Quakerism in Seventeenth-Century Massachusetts Bay* (Westport: Greenwood Press, 1985), 140.

through his childhood and adolescent indoctrination as a Congregationalist. The influence of Congregationalism is aptly evidenced through Rogers's view on how men and women could gain entrance to eternal life. The subscription to Calvinism indicated that orthodoxy had taken root in Rogers's psyche and the most influential of sectarians could not deracinate this core doctrine.

The Importance of Education and the Clergy

Beyond the topic of salvation, Congregational beliefs also intertwined with sectarian theology to create unique Rogerene viewpoints on other key topics, such as the role of an educated clergy. Although Rogers denounced the necessity of an erudite leadership, his lauding of educational institutions did not sit well with sectarians who maintained that the learned possessed no advantages compared to the masses. Rogers's intellectual intensity forbade him from censuring the role of education in religion, for he firmly believed that a thriving intellect only enhanced an understanding of God. Rogers commended establishments that aided in the pursuit of spiritual guidance, and therefore spoke well of the proper use of education.

Rogers believed that God's viewpoint of a pauper and priest may be one in the same, and heaven's gate did not discriminate on the basis of wealth, education, or gender. The Congregationalists agreed on this point, as they argued that salvation, which was the free gift of God, could be bestowed upon the most unsuspecting sinner. Yet, there was a slight difference in their observation of equality, as Edmund Morgan points out that Congregationalists believed "salvation was impossible without [education]."[13] Education facilitated a better understanding of God, and Congregationalists maintained that ignorance was man's chief enemy. Hence, any man or woman may be saved but the learned had a better chance of acquiring salvation.

Rogers understood the importance of education but also recognized its limitations. An intellectual understanding of one's religious beliefs was absolutely vital to a well-grounded faith, but education alone

---
[13] Edmund Morgan, *The Puritan Family: Religion and Domestic Relations in Seventeenth-Century New England* (New York: Harper & Row, 1944), 89.

could never produce true spirituality. He stated that "For an orthodox Christian to resolve his Faith into Education, Instruction, and the Perswation of others, is not an higher Reason than a Papist, Mahometan or Pagan, can produce for his Religion."[14] For Rogers, reasoning brought all people, regardless of doctrine, to a certain point of introspection but education could never provide the power of faith needed in the life of a true believer. Therefore, Rogers believed that education was an important foundation to truth but could never convey it in totality.

Rogers's writings reveal a more complex attitude towards a learned ministry than the heretofore-accepted dichotomy of exalted self-learning and denigrated formal education. Rogers did not despise learning institutions or the scholastics offered behind these ivory towers but, rather, the exaggerated preeminence given beyond due recognition. Rogers never promoted ignorance, formal or otherwise, and specifically stated the "unlearned" are apt to be "unstable" and sow to "their own Destruction."[15] Ignorance could equally be remedied in a self-taught manner as in a formal setting; Rogers was merely asserting one was not superior to the other. Rogers's main contention with formal education was the arrogance surrounding the elite, which affected the entire society to some degree.

The avenues to explore one's mind were many and varied, and Rogers asserted that the path that offered formal degrees were no more legitimate than the ones without. Lacking a schoolmaster or educational program, one could learn the tenets of faith through individual studies. A follower of John Rogers confessed that he "never yet seen one Foot within a College Door" but was able to grasp Rogerene tenets through private tutoring and self-contemplation. The most important aspect of religion was the movement of the Spirit that allowed intellectual knowledge to be translated into faith and truth. No amount of education could convince a person to accept knowledge as truth. Borrowing words from the Apostle Paul, Rogerenes believed that "the Wisdom of God" often

---

[14] John Rogers, *An Answer to a Book Intituled, The Lords Day Proved to be the Christian Sabbath &c. By B. Wadsworth, A.M. Pastor of a Church in Boston. And also, An Answer to a Pamphlet, Intituled Thesis concerning the Sabbath. As Also, Some Part of what hath passed through the General Courts in Connecticut Colony, relating to the Sabbath. As Also, Some Court Sentences in that Colony, by John Rogers* (Boston: n.p., 1721), 19.

[15] Rogers, *An Epistle to the Churches of Christ call'd Quakers*, 62.

seems like "foolishness to them that perish," and only the working of the Spirit could attest otherwise.[16]

While it might appear that the more erudite would be the better candidate for teaching parishioners, Rogers pointed to the biblical stories that illustrate God's penchant for "chusing such weak and insufficient Instruments" to "manifest his own Glory." Rogerenes prided themselves in being among the "foolish, weak, base and dispised Things" of the world rather than "the Rev. Assembly of Divines (as they are called)" who "convene at *Westminster*" and teach "Antichristian Principles." Such learned men were seeped in their own pride, and though they taught others, they had an unteachable heart.[17]

While John Rogers was not formally educated at the university level, he was obviously well read in a variety of topics. Rogers was eighteen years old when his father retired from the bakery business. He contemplated following in his father's profession but became a shoemaker instead. In his free time John Rogers spent his days studying theology and law and was known as the scholar of the family. Even without a college degree, Rogers was regarded as a learned man. He ably penned his father's deeds and business documents, and, later, his published writings revealed his extensive knowledge of world history, philosophy, and various theologies.

Rogers's comprehension of religious doctrines was vast. He demonstrated his knowledge by referencing a host of beliefs apart from his own. Extending beyond the beliefs of those in his immediate community, Rogers wrote about past doctrines he found to be erroneous. Starting with the life of Nicolas and "doctrine of the Nicolaitans," Rogers also studied the destruction of the Roman Empire and the ascendancy of Constantine. Rogers continually evaluated religious and secular histories to find meaning in his present world and would often make references to God's judgment in bygone centuries as potential events in his lifetime. For example, Rogers took the rise of Constantine as an act of "God's judgment upon the wicket, to their utter overthrow," as the Almighty would do to the Congregationalists.[18] Rogers also looked at

---
[16] John Bolles, *An Answer of Confutation upon the Articles of the Confession of Faith* (New London: n.p., 1731), i-ii.
[17] Ibid., ii.
[18] John Rogers, *The Book of the Revelation of Jesus Christ, which God gave unto him: to show unto his ser-*

the "destruction of old Babylon, by the Medes and Persians" as a potential parallel of overthrowing established institutions in his day.[19]

The world's fascination with learned institutions symbolized for Rogers a misalignment of priorities. People's desire for "instruction from the wise and learned men, whom they did adore" began to supersede their yearning to "fellowship with God's spirit." As education expanded beyond its intellectual bonds and seeped into spirituality, learned men, whom Rogers called "intruders," entered "into the sheepfold" and became "persecutors of God's" truth. They delivered messages of their own imaginations and "not from the mouth of the Lord."[20] What these ministers taught was problematic, "for they did not expect nor believe any immediate call from God." Real teachers, in comparison, were taught by Christ directly, "and teacheth the righteousness which is of faith, and is written in the heart by the spirit, and are not letter teachers without the spirit. Now all that are in covenant with Christ, are all immediately taught by him."[21] The immediate teachings referenced in such passages once again points to the centrality of Scripture. Though no longer on earth in physical form, Jesus, Rogers believed, continued to teach his followers through the pages of Scripture.

Looking at the life of Christ, Rogers pointed out that Jesus was an unlearned "tradesman, viz. a carpenter" whom the learned men hassled for "going into the meetinghouse to teach." These fake teachers "were wise learned men, not brought up to trades, or work, but to learning, to the end that they might be able to teach others." While Rogers applauded their educational achievements, he condemned false teachers for their unwillingness to do any real work to support themselves. "They are such stewards as cannot work for their living, and to beg they are ashamed, for they are the learned men of the world." These teachers were no better than "thieves, robbers, or hirelings" for laying such a

---

vants things which were to come to pass; and Jesus Christ sent and signified it by his angels to his servant John; and now by revelation, hath opened the mystery contained in said book, unto his servant John Rogers, of his Church and People, after a long and dark night of apostacy. The explanation being made so plain, that they eye of every spiritual reader may see how exactly things have come to pass, as were foretold by the Prophecy of this Book: and may see by it all things which are yet to come, not only to the end of this World but to the finishing of the World to come (Boston: n.p., 1720), 50.
[19] Ibid., 73-74.
[20] John Rogers, *John Rogers a Servant of Jesus Christ, to any of the Flock of Christ that may be scattered among the Churches of New-England, Greeting*, 4th ed. (Norwich: n.p., 1776), 23.
[21] Ibid., 28-30, 35.

"heavy burden on the people" in the form of compulsory taxes. Yet, despite his railings against the misuse of education, Rogers never explicitly condemned learning nor denigrated its place in a person's development.[22]

As a sectarian, Rogers was unusual in that he emphasized the necessity of intellectually understanding one's faith. Feelings and experiences were insufficient in gaining a comprehensive realization of God according to Rogers, and this assertion perhaps caused would-be dissenters to look to the Quakers or Sabbatarians rather than the Rogerenes for fellowship. Moreover, those who denounced Congregationalism but upheld the importance of learning and exercising of the intellect were more likely to join the Baptists than the Rogerenes. The Baptists maintained the importance of a learned ministry and were deemed as sectarians with greater respect and legitimacy than most New England religious dissenters.

The importance of education was clearly noted in Rogers's writing as was its gross misuses. The Congregational church's core issues stemmed from the learned men's exploitation of their status, according to Rogers. Forced tax rates to pay for the minister's salary, elaborate attires and highly decorated induction ceremonies, and their daily pomp in attitude and speech contributed to the obstruction of truth being preached to their congregants. All New England inhabitants were required to pay for their local minister's rates, which Rogers argued was contrary to New Testament examples. The only biblical illustrations of a paid or partially supported ministry were traveling preachers, hence Rogers believed only those in the traveling ministry should be given some monetary compensation.[23] Like the apostles in the New Testament, Rogers believed ministers and clergymen should be self-supporting and not a drain on their communities. Leading by example, Rogers supplemented his ministerial role with his shoemaking practice, and successive Rogerene leaders followed suit. John Rogers, Jr., John Rogers III, John Bolles, Timothy Waterous and Jonathan Whipple were successful craftsmen, weavers, millers, builders

---

[22] Ibid.
[23] Rogers's view on itinerant preaching started during his Sabbatarian days. After Rogers invited Elder Hiscox and Mr. Hubbard to Great Neck for a speaking engagement, he paid them for their services and explained his theology behind his actions. Bolles and Williams, *The Rogerenes*, 139.

and inventors, as well as preachers.[24]

Rogerenes especially loathed the wigs worn by Congregational ministers. Looking at 1 Corinthians 11:4-5, Rogers explained how *"Every man praying or prophecying, having his head covered, dishonoureth his head."* Worse than a man with long hair, according to Rogers, was a man who shamefully covered his head "in the presence of God and his Church." Apart from pageantry, Rogers believed wig-wearing violated Scriptural commands for men to keep their heads uncovered. Rogers took this portion of Scripture literally because symbolically men represented the head of Christ and leaders of their home and community. Rogers assumed these roles very seriously and eschewed any practices that might disqualify his appointment.

Rogers explained his thoughts on wig wearing, but Congregationalists viewed his action as crazed antics. Outwardly Rogers seemed a bit off-kilter as he often followed the local minister throughout town shouting "dost thou think that they wear white wigs in heaven?" When Rogers's pestering became too much he would be fined or forced to sit in the stocks for duration of the day.[25]

Apart from wigs, the general attire of Congregational ministers failed to meet Rogerene standards. Rogers believed clothing "that is decent in God's sight at one time, is decent at all times." It appeared to Rogers the special clothing of Congregational ministers amounted to nothing but materialism and outward display of holiness, much like the Pharisees whom Jesus detested in the Gospels. To be thorough, Rogers did explain rare exceptions when men would be dressed differently from daily activities and from worship. Only citing two such cases in Scripture, Rogers believed Moses and Joshua were the two exceptions as they "were commanded to take off the garment of the feet when they came before God." Otherwise, Rogerenes' dress remained uniform throughout the week and on all occasions. To do otherwise was nothing less than self-aggrandizement and a deviation from the Scriptures.[26]

---

[24] Ellen Starr Brinton, "The Rogerenes," *New England Quarterly* 16, no. 1 (1943): **8.**
[25] George L. Clark, A *History of Connecticut: Its People and Institutions* (New York: G.P Putnam's Sons, 1914), 142.
[26] Rogers, *A Mid-Night Cry from the Temple of God*, 145-49.

The Holy Spirit

Rogers's assessment of education and the proper role of church leaders were not the only issues where he assumed a stance somewhere between Congregational and sectarian principles. His exposition on the Trinity and the role of Scripture also highlight an in-between viewpoint. In Rogers's mind, the mysterious working of the Spirit was closely associated with the doctrine of inner light, and his ideas on the third part of the Trinity were interspersed throughout many of his writings. Although the mystical and indescribable aspects of an elusive deity are hard to make tangible, Rogers did his best through the sense by which he purported to have experienced the Spirit. Rogers wrote at length about the ways he heard, felt, and saw the Spirit at work around him.

Rogerenes have long been regarded as standing members of the religious dissenters who trumped immediate revelation over Scripture. Among their more famous cohort was Anne Hutchinson who was banished from Massachusetts for confessing to hearing from God through immediate revelation. Congregationalists deemed this view as heretical and profane, the same characteristics they attributed to the Rogerenes. Congregationalists and contemporary historians alike, however, have erroneously categorized Rogerenes as part of this group. While John Rogers did in fact believe in immediate revelation, his thoughts on the matter greatly differed from mystics who preceded him. Rogers's definition of "immediate revelation" seemed to differ radically from those attributed by others as his explanation revealed more of an intellectual thought process than a heavenly vision or dreamlike-trance. Moreover, his writings on the subject never denigrated the role of Scripture in the life of a Christian but illustrated its careful weaving with immediate revelation to create a dynamic understanding of God.

Immediate revelation mandates a source of disclosure, and many mystics believed that the one unveiling the directives was God. John Rogers was more precise in defining God's role in immediately revealing instruction as he focused on one part of the Trinity. Unlike some sectarians, such as the Sabbatarians, Rogers agreed with the Congregationalists and supported the validity of the Trinity. The Sabbatarians believed the Father was the Supreme God-head and the Son and Spirit were lesser entities. Rogers regarded the Son and Spirit as co-equals with the Father on all accounts, whether in omniscience, omnipresence, or omnipotence. Rogers claimed "the only one true God, distinguished into Three" are separate entities but one God, for "the Father is a Spirit, the Word is a Spirit, and the Holy Ghost is a Spirit."[27] It was this Holy Ghost, or the Spirit, that Rogers proposed revealed immediate notions into the minds and hearts of believers.

Rogers believed the Spirit's gifts of imparting spiritual understanding, persuasive oration, and discernment of knowledge were bestowed upon people irrespective of the hierarchy structured by man-made laws. The only prerequisite to receiving the Spirit was a willing and obedient heart rather than being born into the privileged class or graduating from a theologically sound institution. Rogers stated, "Thus it appears plainly, that the manifestation of the Spirit is given only to such as obey the call of the Gospel, and so come to receive it by faith."[28] Humility was regarded more highly than the accolades of institutions, which sounded trumpets and raised banners for the learned, the rich, and the privileged – in essence, the proud.

A prime example of the Spirit working in the life of a humble seeker was Rogers's own search for salvation. During his years as a Sabbatarian, Rogers learned the importance of being directed individually and personally by the Spirit. In Rogers's initial years as a Sabbatarian, he was convinced that he must "openly [labour] on the first Day of the Week, in faithfulness to God and my fellow Creature" and submit to the "required rest on the 7th."[29] His actions were dictated through the arguments presented by Sabbatarian leaders, who used Scripture to substantiate their points. Instead of resting content at this conclusion, however, Rogers asked for further enlightenment on the topic. Rogers wanted to understand *why* this directive was given and would not rest until he personally grasped the matter.

Rogers continued to diligently search through the Bible and "beg[ged] at the Throne of Grace for direction in the way of Truth"

---

[27] Ibid., 1-2, 19.
[28] Robers, *An Epistle to the Churches of Christ call'ed Quakers*, 33.
[29] Ibid., vii.

so that he might correctly assess and apply divine directives. It was here that Rogers broke from the Sabbatarians as he realized "that the 7th Day Sabbath was but a Sign (under the Law) of a Gospel Rest that Christ gives the Soul, and that the shadowing part of the Law was nailed to the Cross of Christ."[30] This example reveals two important concepts in the Rogerene view of immediate revelation. First, the Spirit's revelation was not always "immediate." Unearthing the truth had no strict protocol in terms of time; and while the Spirit may reveal an insight through dreams and visions, mostly it was through the process of searching, inquiring, meditating, and thinking. Those processes often took time. Second, the Spirit always worked in conjunction with the written Scriptures. Immediate or processional revelation must always be validated with biblical texts.

Rogers's grappling with Scripture indicated that for him logic was a large part of revelation. Rogers echoed the sentiments of many rationalists in post-Revolutionary America who sought to corroborate religion with reason. He believed that intellectual enlightenment was essential in deepening religious understanding and that the Spirit caused believers to exercise their minds as well as their faiths. Though God's reasoning could elude the human mind at times, Rogerenes believed in striving to understand God through their intellectual capacity.

The intense study of Scripture was a large part of Rogerene life, and much like the Congregationalists, Rogerenes believed in the importance of Scripture to understand God. In fact, much like Congregational preachers of his day, Rogers cross-referenced many biblical texts as he argued "The *best Interpreter* of Scripture, is Scripture, therefore I shall examine into his Place of Scripture, by other Scriptures."[31] It was necessary to comb through the Bible to gain insight into the Almighty's character, and it was through the written text that God still applied guidance to believers. Grasping the Scriptures caused people to exercise their minds, while receiving the text as a personal revelation caused one to exercise their faiths. Rogerenes believed in the importance of combining these forces, as neither could ever successfully stand alone. A faith built solely on immediate revelation caused fanaticism, while one built

---

[30] Ibid., v-vii.
[31] Rogers, *An Answer to a Book Intituled, The Lords Day Proved to be the Christian Sabbath*, 12.

exclusively on intellect was no faith at all.

Rogers made clear that the Scriptures and Spirit were never in opposition but always worked together in the life of a true believer. The authentic working of the Spirit led men and women back to biblical texts to substantiate an insight or revelation. Rogers indicates that the Scriptures confirmed and validated in written form what the Spirit imparted in intangible ways. Rogers confessed that the Spirit "did greatly engage my heart to love God, & diligently to search the Scriptures" and allowed his emotions to turn into an intellectual pursuit of God through written work. Interestingly, he stressed that the motive behind all this searching must never be just a cerebral exercise "but with a purpose in mind; that is, to please God and to serve Him correctly." Those who wanted merely an intellectual insight into God's character could never fully comprehend this deity, for that was the impartation of the Spirit to the obedient and seeking believer. Rogers testified that the "truth" was "confirmed in us, immediately by his Spirit, if we order our conversation aright."[32]

The role of the Spirit was manifold and worked in tandem with Scripture. "Thus it appeareth by the testimony of the Scripture, that this Spirit is the guide of God's Children, and speaketh in them, and sheweth them that it heareth from the Father, and from the Son."[33] One of the Spirit's most salient functions was that of guiding the believer by serving as a tutor to the Scriptures. The Spirit allowed the reader of Scripture to accept biblical texts as fact, and what had merely been intellectual exercise (or what Rogers called "historical faith") would now "become a living faith; for now they are come to know the truth of the Scriptures report."[34] Circularly, the Scriptures justified the Spirit's function of guiding the believer. Rogerenes believed that understanding the Spirit's voice on scriptural matters was essential, otherwise "these Scripture Testimonies" would be open to "any private Interpretation" and "the Earth [would be] covered with Darkness."[35] Although Rogers recognized that a multitude of interpretations could arise from

---

[32] Rogers, *A Mid-Night Cry from the Temple of God*, 127-29.
[33] Ibid., 127.
[34] Ibid., 105-6.
[35] John Rogers, *An Epistle Sent from God to the World, containing the Best News that ever the World Heard. And transcribed by John Rogers, a Servant of Jesus Christ* (New York: Printed for Elisha Stanbury: 1720/1), 24-25.

the same scriptural text, he believed that ultimately there was only one exposition that held true. And he spent his life relentlessly trying to prove why, through the guidance of the Spirit, his interpretations of Scripture held true.

Chapter 5

Methods and Matters of Dissent

Protesting in Print

Hearty demonstrations in public places were the most obvious and noted Rogerene mode of dissent, and they have caught the attention of their contemporaries and current historians alike. Much has been written about these ostentatious displays of protest, and these actions secured them a place in history as rioters, enthusiasts, and liberals. What is not widely known is that Rogerenes employed other modes of dissent quite adeptly. Print and legal protests generally took precedence before physical demonstrations. The Rogerenes used a variety of means to publicize that the Congregationalists were unlawfully situated as the state-sanctioned church, with nonphysical coercion adopted as the first line of defense. Loud and visible protests were always a last resort.

Written protests took on a variety of forms, since the Rogerene leaders were literate and capable of accessing various New England printers. Publishing his views was a means for John Rogers to contend against the Congregationalists for the minds of New Londoners. Rogers endeavored to expose the errors behind Congregational precepts, thereby invalidating their position as the state-sanctioned church. In much of his writings, Rogers focused on coercive Congregational methodologies, such as forced taxation for the meetinghouse and pastoral upkeep, as cause for nullifying state support of Congregationalists. From here, Rogers delved into peripheral reasons, such as wrongful doctrine and corruption of religious leaders, which further augmented his call for censure.

Rogers believed print best publicized Congregational faults in governance and doctrinal beliefs. Congregationalists closely monitored all printed material in New London, and, principally, books were regulated through Congregational standards. And the Congregationalists especially kept an eye on Rogers. In a letter to his friend William Worth "of Nantuckit," Rogers wrote "thy Letter I received" but "the Books I received not." Although the titles of the books are unknown, they appear to have been contrary to Congregational teaching and were confiscated.

Books not in accordance with Congregational teachings were not only confiscated but also burned publicly. Rogers complained that Congregationalists persecuted the "Children of God" by burning their literature and allowing Satan to "suppress the Truth, under pretence of Heresy." Rogers took it as a compliment when his books were burned because he considered himself to be in good company. Rogers compared how "*Luther's* Books" were burned under "pretence utterly to suppress Heresy" and his books, likewise, "have been condemned and burnt, under pretence of heresy." It was only after the 1708 Toleration Act was passed that Rogerenes freely voiced their opinions in print.[1]

Even before the Toleration Act was passed in 1708, Rogers managed to overcome difficulties and publish his thoughts in print. His son, John Rogers, Jr. was fined in 1697 for distributing inappropriate material, which was most likely a Rogerene pamphlet that had yet to be published.[2] Rogers's official publications began in 1701, and in 1705 he stated, "this is the sixth Book printed for me, in single Volumes." Rogers had the money to seek out other avenues of printing when Congregational law forbade him to do so in New London. Rogers sometimes went to Massachusetts, New York, Rhode Island, or other surrounding colonies where printers were willing to publish his heterodox views.[3]

New London authorities kept vigilant watch on the Rogerenes, especially when John Roger circulated his writings around town. Condemned for being "hettridox [sic] in his opinions and practice," Rogers was barred from sharing his theology in print.[4] Rogers traveled to

---

[1] John Rogers, *A Mid-Night Cry from the Temple of God to the Ten Virgins Slumbering and Sleeping, Awake, Awake, Arise, and gird your Loyns, and trim your Lamps, for behold the Bridegroom cometh, go ye therefore out to meet him* (New London: Green, 1722), 16, 176-79.

[2] John Rogers, Jr. was initially bound in prison by the Superior Court for this act. A copy of the unlicensed pamphlet is no longer available but its contents were noted. What filled its pages was the cruel treatment Rogers, Sr. endured by Congregationalists. Rogers, Jr. was released during the October session of the Superior Court but sent back due to his affiliation with William Wright. Wright was their former Native American servant, also known as Japhet, who had been baptized with the Rogers family initially into Sabbatarian principles and acquired a new name. Wright was held in prison for purportedly desecrating the Stonington meetinghouse with "filth." John R. Bolles and Anna B. Williams, T*he Rogerenes: Some Hitherto Unpublished Annals Belonging to the Colonial History of Connecticut* (Boston: Stanhope Press, 1904), 193.

[3] Rogers, *A Mid-Night Cry from the Temple of God*, 16, 176-79.

[4] John R. Bolles and Anna B. Williams, *The Rogerenes: Some Hitherto Unpublished Annals Belonging to the Colonial History of Connecticut* (Boston: Stanhope Press, 1904), 55.

neighboring colonies to get his words on paper, but that all changed when Thomas Short established the first printing press in New London in 1709. This could be seen as a victory for both the sectarians and Standing Order since both sides used print to defend their cause. The difference, of course, was that the Congregational authorities had official control over what could and could not be printed.

The intricacies and depth of Rogerene doctrine were shared with New Londoners through oral dissemination and print distribution. Rogerenes held public meetings where all inhabitants were invited to listen to sermons and engage in religious discourse. Many such exchanges occurred throughout John Rogers's leadership, and Congregationalists, Baptists, Quakers, and Sabbatarians are mentioned in a handful of these meetings. Many of John Rogers's thoughts on doctrine, as well as on government and society, were recorded in his writings. Each book reveals a unique aspect of Rogers's personal life and how he reconciled ideals with reality. McLoughlin notes that Rogerenes seized every available opportunity to publish their views and challenge Congregationalists in print. These writings certainly had an impact on New London culture between the late seventeenth and early eighteenth centuries and were "as pungent as anything written by Roger Williams or George Fox."[5] How widely Rogerene books were distributed in and beyond New London is uncertain but what remains definitive is that Rogerene literature caught the attention of their immediate inhabitants and local authorities.

As noted by David D. Hall, printers played an important role in colonial life. While their licenses were managed by the Standing Order, they tried to make their businesses prosper whenever possible. Printers made themselves available to all sorts of topics because they were after all entrepreneurs.[6] Of course Congregationalists cracked down on written treatises they deemed offensive and hoped to stamp out such troublesome behavior. But people with deviant ideas were able to find printers who believed the dollar to be mightier than the law.

Not surprisingly, often legal reprimands only incited more unrest as Congregationalists punished printed assaults on ecclesiastical or

---

[5] William G. McLoughlin, *New England Dissent, 1630-1833: The Baptists and the Separation of Church and State* (Cambridge: Harvard University Press, 1971), I:251.
[6] David D. Hall, *Worlds of Wonder, Days of Judgment: Popular Religious Belief in Early New England* (Cambridge: Harvard University Press, 1989), 22.

governmental institutions. As Congregational admonishments continued, the Rogerenes responded with even more aggressive tactics to disseminate their ideas on paper. One of Rogers's choice weapons for disturbing Congregational worship was penning treatises deriding clerical leaders, which were often fixed on the door of the New London meeting house. Much like Luther had nailed his *95 Theses* on the doors of the Castle Church in Wittenberg, Rogers posted scathing diatribes upon the meetinghouse doors in hopes that all church attendees would have their eyes opened to the "popish" ordinances of Congregational leaders.[7]

One example of such a written protest was in 1677, when James, Sr., his wife Elizabeth Rogers, James, Jr., Jonathan Rogers, John Rogers, and Bathshua Smith were each fined £5 for posting a "scandalous paper" on the doors of the New London meetinghouse. Most of the material in this circulation aimed at persuading their readers to view the state-sanctioned church as illegitimate. Exposing errors in theology and abuses in power would prove that the Congregationalists were obviously the "false" church. Only "true" churches, or religious institutions advocating correct theology, should be upheld by the state, according to Rogers. Of course what constituted correct theology was a highly contested debate in colonial days. Ultimately, each Rogerene paid the £5 fine without contention.[8]

Another example of written protest came at the special court in New London on January 24, 1694 to consider a case against Richard Steer, Samuel Beebe, Jr., Jonathan Rogers, and James Rogers, Jr. for writing papers accusing the government of causing colonialists to violate English law. This essay, too, was posted on the doors of the New London meetinghouse. Specifically, Rogerenes wrote a treatise that argued that to compel people to pay for a "Presbyterian" minister is against the law of England and just plain robbery and oppression.[9] The court fined each petitioner £5 for their written protests, and the Court of Assistants at Hartford confirmed the initial decision after Rogerenes had appealed. Though a few Rogerenes threatened to take the matter to the

---
[7] Francis Manwaring Caulkins, *History of New London, Connecticut: From the First Survey of the Coast in 1612, to 1860* (New London: H.D. Utley, 1895), 213.
[8] Ibid., 206.
[9] The Rogerenes often referred to the Congregationalists as Presbyterians due to the changes in governance that appeared to be structured into a presbytery rather than autonomous local churches.

throne of England, actual prosecution never transpired.[10]

As the leader of a dissenting faction in New England, John Rogers expended great energy in attempting to display the differences between the true and false churches. And print was often the choice method of disseminating this comparison. He was obsessed with proving why the predominant religion of Congregationalism was in fact the false church that Scripture refers to as "Heathen[s] that know [God] not."[11] Rogers argued that the false church led many unsuspecting men and women astray through their faulty interpretation of scriptural precepts, and, broadly speaking, they missed the mark by inappropriately observing private elements of the religious life. In areas where privacy should have been emphasized, such as prayer and meditation, Rogers contended that Congregationalists made them into public spectacles devoid of true worship.

Full submission to biblical teaching mandated that Rogerenes dutifully "put these things to publick view" and alert the masses to Congregational mendacity. Rogerenes fought against "the Wiles of Satan," who earnestly desired to "mis-lead" men by forcing them "to make Idols of such things which God commanded to be observed as signs of Instructions to his Church."[12] As the keeper of truth, Rogers took it upon himself to compare Congregational teaching with what he considered as veritable and reasonably display why his interpretation should prevail. Rogerene leaders made it a point to thoroughly understand the doctrines of other religions and especially those of the Congregationalists. Rogerene riots were based on a firm understanding of what they were opposing, and the firm grasp of competing theologies is most notable in print protests lobbied by Rogerenes. Rogers and later generations of Rogerene leaders were incredibly deliberate in their assessment of differing beliefs. For example, Rogers's dissection of the Congregational Confession of Faith was thorough and lucid. His comments revealed the authorship of a man who had spent a vast amount of time pondering Congregational doctrine. Interestingly, Rogers's assessment appears evenhanded and unbiased, even offering commendation toward

---

[10] Caulkins, *History of New London*, 213.
[11] John Rogers, *An Epistle to the Churches of Christ call'd Quakers; And another epistle to the Seventh Day Baptists, with several Theological Essays* (New York: William Bradford, 1705), 80-81.
[12] Ibid., ix.

some Congregational practices. Though he had problems with a variety of doctrinal matters, he stated to Congregationalists that "the said Counsels in the Confession of your Faith is so substantially grounded in the holy Scriptures." Despite their theological differences, Rogers believed that Congregationalism upheld certain tenets that were biblically based.[13]

Rogers challenged Congregational ministers on their knowledge of Scripture and wanted to duel in print. Looking at the issue of the Sabbath, Rogers dared Congregationalist ministers to defend their position and "in the Presence and View of the World, to shew us *Chapter* and *Verse*" for such commands. Further, he asked "to quote to us the Place of Scripture" where they found their commands and "send it to us." Further, he instructed them "if there be no Command of God for it in the Holy Scriptures, and only your own Law in your Law Book and your *Ministers* Doctrine for it, then I desire you to read and to consider what is written, Mat. 15, 7th, 8th, and 9th Verses." After waiting a while, Rogers never received a reply. To their lack of response, Rogers concluded "But I could obtain no Answer from them; *for every one that doth Evil hateth the Light, neither cometh to the Light, lest his Deeds should be discovered.*"[14]

Rogerenes asked Congregationalists to return the favor and be placed under a doctrinal microscope. Far from being left alone, Rogerenes wanted to be the subject of intense scrutiny and rational discourse. Rogers desired that the Congregationalists would understand Rogerene doctrine and systematically debate point-by-point the issues they found contentious. If the Congregationalists could persuade Rogerenes of the errors of their beliefs, this would be far more persuasive than the legal methods used to deter Rogerene worship. Rogers told the Congregationalists that if they could demonstrate the faulty precepts of the Rogerenes, "this will be more for your Honour than to compel us against our own Consciences" by us-

---

[13] John Rogers, *An Answer to a Book Intituled, The Lords Day Proved to be the Christian Sabbath &c. By B. Wadsworth, A.M. Pastor of a Church in Boston. And also, An Answer to a Pamphlet, Intituled Thesis concerning the Sabbath. As Also, Some Part of what hath passed through the General Courts in Connecticut Colony, relating to the Sabbath. As Also, Some Court Sentences in that Colony, by John Rogers* (Boston: n.p., 1721), 23.
[14] Ibid., 22-23.

ing "your Whips, Stocks, Fines and Imprisonments." Rogers found an intellectual debate far more productive and enlightening than physical coercion.[15]

Just as print was used to expose errors in Congregational precepts, Rogers also used this medium to encourage the "true" church to remain vigilant. Encouraging sectarians to view themselves as the "legitimate" church was a protest against the status quo. Believing his followers to be the true church, Rogers exhorted believers to endure hardships meted out by Congregationalists, and Rogers's views on suffering and warfare are especially concentrated in his exposition on the book of Revelation. He used this treatise to encourage fellow believers as they were reviled for their convictions. Believing himself to be living in or just before the end times, Rogers wrote a 262-page commentary on the last book of the Bible. He believed a proper study of this book was necessary to engage in the spiritual battles at Armageddon, and he endeavored to equip his followers by expounding upon chapter by chapter and verse by verse through Revelation. Throughout his commentary, Rogers made numerous analogies between the oppression suffered by true believers in Revelation and the life of the Rogerenes in New London.

Much of his commentary exhorted the Rogerenes to persevere throughout their hardships. Just as the Apostle John, author of Revelation, was heavily persecuted by the authorities of his day, Rogers noted that the Rogerenes were "companions with John in tribulation." Rogers used the Apostle John's longsuffering "as a precedent" for the Rogerenes "to be patient in tribulation, that thereby we may gain experience."[16] As Rogers read through Revelation, he must have noted that the followers of Christ did not find reprieve during their earthly lives. As such, Rogers did not engage in warfare against the Congregationalists to make a better life for himself, his followers, or their off-

---

[15] Ibid., 22.

[16] John Rogers, *The Book of the Revelation of Jesus Christ, which God gave unto him: to show unto his servants things which were to come to pass; and Jesus Christ sent and signified it by his angels to his servant John; and now by revelation, hath opened the mystery contained in said book, unto his servant John Rogers, of his Church and People, after a long and dark night of apostasy. The explanation being made so plain, that they eye of every spiritual reader may see how exactly things have come to pass, as were foretold by the Prophecy of this Book: and may see by it all things which are yet to come, not only to the end of this World but to the finishing of the World to come* (Boston: n.p., 1720), 5-6.

spring. Instead, he unduly warned the Rogerenes of their need to suffer in their present lives without desiring to see rewards until their deaths. Rogers believers that efforts that appeared as useless or vain through immediate circumstances needed to be extended for God's purposes to be fulfilled. Patience was absolutely necessary, as Rogers believed true reckoning would primarily come in the afterlife. The Rogerenes needed to prepare themselves for a lifetime of battle that could only find rest in their deaths or return of Jesus Christ. With such a rationale, Rogerenes could not be dissuaded through adverse circumstances. Therefore, their demonstrations against the Congregationalists were difficult to abate.

Though early living proved difficult at times, Rogers foretold of their glorious end upon Christ's return. On that Day of Judgment, the Rogerenes could claim the promise of Revelation 11:12, where the true church "ascended up to heaven in a cloud, and their enemies beheld them." On this day, those that had been persecuted as "hereticks, pestilent fellows, sowers of sedition, troublers of the commonwealth; yea, esteemed them to be the filth and offscouring of all things" were now the "favorites of heaven, and to be advanced into such a great glory." This would be "a dreadful day for" the false church to behold.[17] Rogers exhorted his followers that the future condemnation of the false church is unworthy to be compared to the earthly hardships suffered by the Rogerenes. Rogers explained in detail the just punishment of the false church, which will be relegated to "the hottest place of hell fire, where they shall ever be Tormented, not only for their actual sins, in transgressing the law of God, but chiefly for their hypocrisie." The leaders of the false church "shall receive the greater Damnation" and "shall be bound hand and foot, and case into outer darkness, [where] there shall be weeping and gnashing of teeth."[18]

Rogers pointed to the political power held by the Congregationalists as proof of their apostasy because in Revelation the false church "sitteth upon many waters" and is known as "Babylon the great." Likening the Congregationalists to this evil empire, Rogers called them "this whore," the "false church, which hath all the power of men and devils

---
[17] Ibid., 109.
[18] Rogers, *A Mid-Night Cry from the Temple of God*, 94-97.

on her side." In contrast, the "true church is described to be in a poor, low, miserable, and perishing state." Looking at the small number of Rogerenes and their inferior position compared to Congregationalists, Rogers argued that they must be the true church. Of course this meant that other sectarians could also claim that they were the true church, but Rogers argues that no other theology was as scripturally sound as his. The false church, in their "great pomp" and "very numerous" members, makes war against the true church by "overcoming them, and killing them; thus wasting and consuming them." Rogers further pointed to the great numbers of persecutions he endured, which was far more than other sectarians, as his badge of honor.[19]

Rogers added the wrongdoings of the government to his warfare treatise as the church and state worked in tandem. Rogers described the state as the main arm of "the Devil and Satan" and noted "the Powers of this World" as synonymous with the governmental order. The false church, "which they have established," are maintained and "upheld" by the state. And, most importantly, the false churches are run by "the false Prophets" and "Ministers which they set up and maintain with great Sums of Money."[20] Congregational ministers kept "in friendship with the judges of the earth" in order to be handsomely paid for their services. Their main goal was to "make an image of worship to the earthly power" and force all, "both small and great, rich and poor, to worship that image."[21]

Rogers vowed to combat this dual combination of church and state regardless of the price. Rogerenes consoled themselves with thoughts about a glorious eternal future when they were reviled by New London authorities. Although Rogers bore the brunt of Congregational persecution, he remained the most steadfast and certain about his rewards for sharing his personal convictions with those in his midst. His leadership was instrumental in bringing about greater diversity in religious beliefs, although that was not his aim. Exercising his personal

---

[19] Rogers, *The Book of the Revelation of Jesus Christ*, 69, 105.
[20] Rogers, *A Mid-Night Cry from the Temple of God*, 7-8.
[21] John Rogers, *John Rogers A Servant of Jesus Christ, To any of the Flock of Christ that may be scattered among the Churches of New-England, Greeting. Giving a description of the True Shepherds of Christ's Flock; and also of the Anti-Christian Ministers; According to the testimony of Jesus Christ and his Apostles, in the Holy Scriptures. As also something touching baptism and the Lord's supper* (Newport: James Franklin, 1754), 29-30.

convictions was a costly choice for Rogers, but he was convinced that there was no other way to live.

Physical Demonstrations

Although the Rogerenes were most notorious for their physical demonstrations, they only resorted to these raucous acts as a final measure. Rogerenes marched into meetinghouses on Sundays only after their print and legal protests fell on deaf ears. And the Rogerenes endured harsh persecution by Congregationalists as these protests escalated throughout John Rogers's tenure as leader. As Rogerenes struggled to make their voice heard, Congregationalists responded with heavy-handed reprimands, and New London ecclesiastical and civil leaders were not amused by Rogerene antics and demonstrations. Some punishments were courted by Rogerenes, as at times they delighted in inviting trouble. For example, on a few occasions, Rogerenes took pride in reporting on themselves when authorities failed to punish them. In fact, John Bolles mentioned his "cheerful spirit" as he "would inform against [himself] before witness[es]" as he worked on the Sabbath. Bathsheba Rogers Smith was also known for interrupting worship at the New London meetinghouse on Sundays to proclaim she had been doing work within the confines of her home.[22]

Other charges and punishments were more serious, such as when the New London meetinghouse burned down in 1695. Rogerenes were charged with suspicion of arson and were arraigned before the Superior Court in Hartford. The Rogerenes were later exonerated after a prolonged series of trials. Though Rogerenes were troublesome, they were upfront about their disturbances and would have gladly taken credit for the fire had they started it. At times, Congregational persecution of Rogerenes was unduly harsh when compared to the crimes committed. Severe persecution only encouraged the Rogerenes to demonstrate more forcefully because they believed legal suffering was a call of duty to all true Christians.[23]

An example of such harsh punishment and counter-Rogerene re-

---
[22] Caulkins, *History of New London, Connecticut*, 204-215.
[23] Rogers, *A Mid-Night Cry from the Temple of God*, 7.

sponse is Rogers's incarceration in 1694. Due to a series of demonstrations against the Sabbath, Rogers was confined for three years and eight months and suffered physical retribution. He described the whips used on him "which [he] knew well," since the whip was kept close to his cell and used in hopes of breeding religious conformity. The two knots at the end of the whip were "about so big as a Walnut" and the officer called to whip Rogers "did the execution" with much force since he "did not only strike with the strength of his arm, but with a swing with his body also." Rogers went on to say that he was given sixty lashes which exceeded the "forty stripes, according to the Law of Moses," and received sixteen additional lashes after he refused to beg for their mercy and instead called them "cruel Wretches." Thereafter, taken to prison, Rogers had "one leg chained to the cill" and "not so much as straw to lie on, nor any covering, the floor was hollow from the ground." He was so chained for six weeks in the dead of winter and given nothing but some dry morsels of bread to eat. The "Gaoler" vowed to make Rogers thankful for the bread and force him to "comply with their Worship."[24]

The ongoing duel between Rogers and New London religious and civil authorities only intensified as the years wore on. His unrepentant attitude caused him to receive harsher penalties than the crimes justified. More often than not, Rogerenes stood to the finish and endeavored to make their point at all costs. There were moments, however, when Rogerenes quietly acquiesced to Congregational laws. Just as Congregational persecution fluctuated, Rogerene response was not uniform. Sometimes Rogerenes fiercely fought back and pushed their nonviolent policy to the edge, as was demonstrated by Rogers's long incarceration. Other examples were nonpayment of fines issued by various courts and the physical removing of livestock from Rogerene acreage as payment. Once, when authorities came to take away a barrel of beef to compensate for their minister's salary, James Rogers, Jr. and his wife assaulted the constable by throwing scalding water on him and successfully recaptured the beef. Other times, Rogerenes quietly relented to fines and payments and willfully surrendered to Congregational mandates. For example, when Bathsheba Fox had the choice of paying £10 or be severely whipped for profaning the Sabbath, the fine was opted for

[24] Ibid., 13-16.

over the flogging. Also, when John Rogers, Jr. was placed under bond for trial, Samuel Rogers paid for his release and no further mention of that case remains on file.[25]

Regardless of the method of protest, Rogerenes faced persecution from civil and religious authorities. The civil government in New London took the liberty of defining "rioting" as they wished and often cited Rogerenes for such being disturbers of the peace. Rogers complained that any actions whatsoever that did not sit well with the governmental leaders were dubbed as disorderly. Rogers deemed as an unjust censure, for example, an incident where he was fined ten shillings for using the meetinghouse to discuss biblical passages. He purposefully chose dinnertime so that the meetinghouse would be empty, and, still, he was not allowed to use this facility. Later, Rogers took his Bible study outside the New London meetinghouse to discuss Rogerene doctrine with those standing-by but was fined for this act. Undoubtedly Congregationalists viewed Rogers's proselytizing as leading astray the inhabitants.

In another instance, he was reprimanded for sitting in the New London meetinghouse when it was empty. It is unclear if Rogers sat in his pre-bought seat or in a general seat, but either should not have incited reprisal since meetings or worship were not in session. Rogers stated, "I went into no other Seat but that which I was seated in, by them whom the Town appointed to seat every one." He was mediating and praying in the meetinghouse when authorities fined him for trespassing.[26]

Forced to pay for the building and upkeep of the meetinghouse, Rogers felt entitled to its usage. Implying extortion, Roger stated that he gave "Three of the best fat Cattle I had that year" to help build the meetinghouse. Further, he was required to give thirty shillings from his shoe business to augment the meetinghouse funds. These were compulsory tithes since Rogers refused initial payment and was charged an additional ten shillings for noncompliance. In lieu of the ten shillings, an officer confiscated ten sheep, which Rogers complained were worth more than the fine. To add insult to injury, the authorities confiscated additional animals, which resulted in double payment of that initial ten-shilling fine. After the sheep were sold, Rogers stated that "the Officer went

---

[25] Bolles and Williams, *The Rogerenes*, 185.
[26] Ibid., 25.

into My Sons Pasture unbeknown to him, and took a Milch cow" in addition to all that was already taken. These were fraudulent confiscations in Rogers's mind, and they were nothing new to the Rogerenes. Rogers maintain that such acts had "frequently [been] done upon us" and he could have listed innumerable similar accounts but refrained for the sake of brevity. Rogers said that great volumes could be composed from all that the Rogerenes had suffered for their religious convictions. As long as true justice eluded their grasp, Rogerenes were committed to fighting against Congregational authorities with all their might.[27]

Although there are many events that capture Rogerene punishment, the next example highlights the harshest penalties faced by this sect. Rogers was imprisoned for demonstrating on the Sabbath in November 1712, and, thereafter, he refused to pay a bond for his release. Upon his refusal, Rogers was sent to prison under extremely harsh conditions. Rogers noted that Congregational bystanders were appalled by his maltreatment, although he did not belong to their beliefs. Gurdon Saltonstall endeavored to keep Rogers locked up in a cold cell during a "violent cold Winter" that his "Blood was so chill'd and jellied with the Cold." His maltreatment caused the "Town [to be] raised" and even some Congregationalists responded with friendly gestures. Rogers happily noted that even the New London minister Eliphalet Adams sent him a *"Bottle of Spirits"* and his wife sent her sympathies. He was touched by their "Kindness," which he felt obligated to acknowledge in print. Likewise, a handful of Congregationalists offered their condolences. Rogers was moved by these "Neighbors [who] came about" him with words and "what Relief they could" in the form of food items or clothing.[28]

At the ill treatment of his father, John Rogers, Jr. made a ruckus and "ran along the Street, crying *the Authority hath killed my Father.*" For this, Rogers, Jr. was fine for "making a Rant in the Night." Rogers, Jr. asked to be tried by a jury. The jury was rigged, according to Rogers, as Saltonstall dismissed the random selection of jurors and "pannell'd a Jury purposely for him." This new jury found Rogers, Jr. guilty of "ranting" and charged him three cows worth of fines. Upon

---

[27] Ibid., 25-26.
[28] Rogers, *An Answer to a Book Intituled, The Lords Day proved to be the Christian Sabbath*, 26.

issuance of the fine, local authorities promptly took the three best cows in Rogers, Jr.'s pasture.[29]

After a cold night in the cell, Rogers's case was dismissed and set about going home when the sheriff, who was also the tavern keeper, requested Rogers's company at the tavern. This was a decoy to keep Rogers detained as the sheriff told Rogers "the Superior Court had ordered him to shut me up." When Rogers demanded a written order for this arraignment, the sheriff said it had been given to him "by Word of Mouth." When the local townspeople heard this exchange, they spoke on behalf of Rogers. There were many present who told [the sheriff], *"he ought not to shut me up without a written Order."* The sheriff "then laid violent Hands on" Rogers to incarcerate him, "but the People rescued me." Later, a written order was given by the court to keep Rogers in prison. The sheriff brought back "this following *Mittimus*" which stated by the "special Order" to:

> take John Rogers Senior of new London, who to the View of said Court, appears to be under an high Degree of Distraction, and him secure in her Majesty's Goal for the County aforesaid, the same dark Room or Apartment thereof, that proper Means may be used for his Cure, and till he be recover'd from his Madness and [there is an] Order for his Release.

Rogers was taken off to the dark prison where "the Light of the Window stopt." When the townspeople heard of the darkness, once again they interceded on Rogers's behalf. "Upon this the common People was in an Uproar, and broke the Plank of the Window and let Light in." The reaction of the spectators reveals that extreme circumstances could bridge religious differences. Many of the watchers were non-Rogerenes and they emphatically spoke out for the civil rights of these sectarians. Congregationalists, however, did not consistently express outrage for sectarians, and it was unusual for the town's minister to sympathize with a religious dissident.[30]

After some unspecified time, Rogers was taken to the sheriff's house and placed under house arrest. No one was guarding him, so Rog-

---
[29] Ibid.
[30] Ibid., 27-28.

ers took the opportunity to flee. He justified this action by explaining they were going to "see me shut up in some dark Room, and that one Laboreel French Doctor was to shave my head, and give me Purges to recover me of my Madness." Rogers ran away to Long Island and endeavored to find justice through their courts. He went to see the "Justice to give him an Account of the Matter," but all he said was "It is the Sabbath, it is not a Day to Discourse about such things." Interestingly, Rogers returned to the tavern where he had been kept a prisoner. Why he went back is uncertain. Upon his return, he was re-imprisoned, now with a guard set to watch over him. He noticed that "three Justices" were waiting for him with a "written Paper lying before them, and read a Law to me, *That it was to be counted Felony, to break out of a Constables Hand.*"[31]

There seems to be gaps in his testimony since Rogers was able to secure his release again thereafter. He brought his case before one of the "officers of York" who "advised me to go for England, and make my Complaint, and told me there was a Ship then going from Pensilvania." And someone even offered to lend him money for his passage even if he could not repay it. Roger sentimentally noted "All this Kindness have I met with from Strangers." During Rogers's stay in New York for about three months, he was sought after in New London. Later, Rogers found a wanted poster out for him, which urged "all Persons to seize and secure the said Rogers and return him forthwith unto me the Subscriber, sheriff of the said County, and they shall be well satisfied for the Trouble and Charge they may be at therein. Dated in New-London, March 31st 1721." Rogers went to the "Printer to know who it was that drew this *Advertisement* up, and he shewed me the Copy, and I took it to be Governour Saltonstall's own Hand."[32]

Rogers's seemingly crazed antics might find some rationale in his military analogy. He sincerely believed he was in a state of war against Congregationalists, who constituted the "false Church" and "false Prophets." Rogerene principles barred physical warfare but not

---

[31] Ibid., 28.
[32] Gurdon Saltonstall, *A Sermon Preached before the General Assembly of the Colony of Connecticut at Hartford in New England, May 13, 1697, being the Day for Electing the Governour, Depty Governour and Assistants, for that Colony* (Boston: B. Green and J. Allen, 1697), 5-6.

spiritual ones. Rogers called himself a "listed Soldier" for Christ, mature in service "now about thirty two years" when this treatise was published in 1705.[33] This would have made John Rogers fifty-seven years old at the time of publication. Counting backwards, this meant Rogers considered himself a true soldier of Christ starting from 1673, the year prior to his joining the Sabbatarians. Even if this piece was written earlier than the published date, which was very well likely, this undergirds Rogers's belief that he became an authentic follower of Christ once he left the Congregational fold and embarked on his journey toward a more individualistic faith.

For scriptural reasons, Rogers refused to engage in physical warfare, which he differentiated from physical demonstrations. Rogerenes denounced the usage of weapons, for Jesus taught his disciples that "All they that take the Sword shall perish by the Sword; and He that killeth with the Sword must be killed with the Sword." Rogers stated "it is an evil Thing for a Christian to practice any Gesture that tendeth to War, as watching, warding or training, or exercising any Posture leading to War." War was evil because "it is some Degree of Contempt to the Doctrine of Christ, who hath taught us to learn War no more, but to live the Life of Faith and Love, who hath promised us his Protection and Preservation from Famine, Pestilence and Sword, when we love him and keep his Commandments." Instead of taking up the sword, Christ taught "to beat their Swords into useful Tools, for necessary Uses." Rogerenes took this to heart and acquired skills that made them productive members in society.[34]

Rogerenes viewed Congregational persecutions as intense spiritual warfare. They categorized the use of "Prisons, Stocks, Whips, Fines and Revilings" as "the Sword of the Devil's Spirit to defend Doctrines of Devils."[35] The countless pages of persecution need not be recited verbatim for Rogers concluded that "it would contain a Book of a large Volume to" merely relate what he "Suffered in the time of this Imprisonment."[36] Themes and motives, however, behind the suffering do need appraisal for they shed light upon the orthodox

---
[33] Rogers, *A Mid-Night Cry from the Temple of God*, 5-8.
[34] Rogers, *John Rogers A Servant of Jesus Christ*, 17.
[35] Caulkins, *History of New London*, 212.
[36] Rogers, *A Mid-Night Cry from the Temple of God*, 13-15.

and unconventional psyches of New Londoners alike.

Roger spent many years in a self-proclaimed war against the Congregationalist, and he firmly believed that spiritual warfare must translate into physical acts. He justified his loud demonstrations as part of a holy war that often landed him in prison. He led the Rogerene crusade that exposed errors in Congregational practices, regardless of the price he was forced to pay. Surprisingly, in the final years of Rogers's his life, his treatises on demonstrations and violating Congregational laws eased somewhat. The reasoning for this change of heart can be found in the last of his writings.

In one of Rogers's last published books, *John Rogers, A Servant of Jesus Christ, to all my beloved Brethren in Christ, Greeting*, there is a lengthy rationale for his pacifist ideals. Rogerenes were always against oath taking and waging war, but this book indicates that Rogerenes were tilting towards a less abrasive approach in their demonstration against the Congregational order. This book was broken up into three segments, where the first two parts elaborated on Rogerene theories on traditional medicine, the duty of ministers, and oath taking. The third section, "Concerning the Second or Gospel Ministration," is definitely a pronouncement against war and might be the first official commitment of John Rogers and his followers to abstain from any form of violent demonstrations. After the publication of this book and henceforth, there is considerably less interference with the law and this may well be due to the ideas printed in this book.

Rogerenes demonstrated heartily against Congregational laws but their affronts were not haphazard or without reason. Though John Rogers disagreed with the number of ecclesiastical and civil mandates prescribed by Congregationalists, he believed that the issues which undercut a person's spiritual individualism and intellectual reasoning were the most problematic. And the Rogerenes endeavored to employ any means necessary to reveal why these rites particularly threatened a personal and rational faith. The many laws, both ecclesiastical and civil, that governed colonial life could not have met the satisfaction of all New London inhabitants. The difference for Rogers was that he made his displeasure known and refused to comply with laws he deemed antithetical to his personal convictions and against the laws of Scripture. As a man devoted to the "inerrant Word of God," Rogers felt that acquiescing to laws that he deduced to be contrary to God's own would violate his allegiance to the highest authority. Church and state in Rogers's eyes were inferior institutions when compared to God's kingdom.

Chapter 6

Family Matters

A Landmark Case

The union between John Rogers and Elizabeth Griswold Rogers was no ordinary marriage. She was his first and most beloved wife and the woman who greatly shaped his views on the role of women in the church, in the home, and in the community. Initially, Elizabeth Griswold Rogers had shared in her husband's beliefs when he openly adopted Sabbatarian views. During those years, she encouraged Rogers to interact with other Sabbatarians and aided her husband in searching the Scriptures to validate Sabbatarian principles. She witnessed a transformation taking place within her husband and desired a renewed spirit herself.[1] She started attending Sabbatarian meetings and no longer worshipped with Congregationalists at the New London meetinghouse. Before her baptism could confirm her Sabbatarian membership, however, her parents intervened.

Matthew and Anna Griswold thought that their daughter was duped by such madness and desperately tried to expose the flaws of her new beliefs. In later writings, John Rogers, Jr. claimed that his maternal grandmother was the central reason for his parents' divorce because she incited a rift between the couple. Openly siding with his father, John Rogers, Jr. accused his maternal grandmother of being "the main Instrument which Satan at length made use of to deceive J.R.'s Wife" by "giving her Daughter an account of her own Conversion" and "telling her Daughter there was no such great change in the Work of Conversion, as they had met with."[2] Essentially Anna Griswold made clear her belief that Rogers's immediate revelations were nothing more than delusional

---

[1] John R. Bolles and Anna B. Williams, *The Rogerenes: Some Hitherto Unpublished Annals Belonging to the Colonial History of Connecticut* (Boston: Stanhope Press, 1904), 128.
[2] John Rogers, Jr., *An Answer to a Book Lately Put Forth by Peter Pratt, Entituled, The Prey Taken from the Strong. Wherein by Mocks and Scoffs, together with a great number of positive Falshoods, the Author hath greatly abused John Rogers, late of New-London, deceased, since his Death* (New York: n.p., 1726), 34.

antics cooked up to create trouble.³

After countless hours of discussion spanning the course of a few months, Anna Griswold finally succeeded in turning her daughter's mind back to Congregationalism. Elizabeth Griswold Rogers "soon publickly recanted, and renounced that Spirit which she had been led by, and declared it to be the Spirit of the Devil." Though elated with their daughter's return to orthodoxy, the Griswolds would not be satisfied unless Rogers denounced Sabbatarianism as well. They hoped their daughter could convince Rogers of the errors of Sabbatarianism and return to the Congregational way.⁴

The months following Elizabeth Griswold Rogers's return to Congregationalism were emotionally trying for Rogers as he listened to the arguments and desperate pleas of his dear wife on many occasions. She reminded her husband that they were still "members of the regular church" and "their two children have been baptized in that church, at New London." Their "good and regular standing" at the Congregational Church would devolve into "disgrace unspeakable" should they continue their deviant course.⁵ Elizabeth Griswold Rogers "then vehemently perswaded her Husband to [repent]; telling him with bitter Tears, that unless he would renounce that Spirit, she dare not live with him."⁶ Her entreaties turned to threats as she sensed Rogers's unyielding stance on the matter; and by the end of 1674, her threats became a reality as she left their home on Mamacock farm with both their children in tow. She rejoined her parents in Blackhall along with two-year-old Elizabeth, Jr. and infant John, Jr.⁷

Elizabeth Griswold Rogers applied for divorce in May of 1675 on the grounds of heterodoxy and "certain alleged immoralities."⁸ She had hoped for reconciliation before this point, but she finally concluded that Rogers would never denounce his new sect and return to the

---

³ Often John Rogers, Jr. used additional testimony by neighbors or friends to corroborate his story. In this instance, he cited Daniel Stubbins and Mary Tubs, "two of [the Griswolds'] next Neighbours," to confirm his claim that Mrs. Matthew Griswold was the main cause for contention between John and Elizabeth Rogers. Rogers, Jr., *An Answer to a Book Lately Put Forth by Peter Pratt*, 34-35.
⁴ Rogers, Jr., *An Answer to a Book Lately Put Forth by Peter Pratt*, 34-36.
⁵ Bolles and Williams, *The Rogerenes*, 127-29.
⁶ Rogers, Jr., *An Answer to a Book Lately Put Forth by Peter Pratt*, 35.
⁷ Bolles and Williams, *The Rogerenes*, 128-129.
⁸ Frances Manwaring Caulkins, *History of New London, Connecticut: From the First Survey of the Coast in 1612, to 1860* (New London: H.D. Utley, 1895), 208.

Congregational church. The alleged wrongdoings on Rogers's part were extremely serious charges raised by Elizabeth Griswold Rogers. She claimed that her issuance of divorce was in part "on the account of his Beastiality."[9] Court records indicate that these allegations were dropped due to insufficient evidence and that they were never taken all that seriously in the first place. Though Rogers was exonerated from the bestiality charge, the claim of heterodox views remained, and the divorce was finalized at the October 12, 1676 session of the General Court in Hartford. A subsequent act of the Assembly, on October 1677, gave her full custody of their two children.[10]

The Rogers's divorce was a landmark case. When the courts granted Elizabeth Griswold custody of her two children, she earned a place in American history as a woman who set legal precedence. Court records indicate that this was "probably the first American case in which courts granted custody to the mother." Nearly two decades later, Mercy Hill, another divorcée, was granted custody of her two children in 1692. Although this case was considered less highly charged than the Rogers case, Ebenezer Hill, Mercy Hill's adulterous husband, lost all rights to parental authority for his "serious moral breach." These two cases are considered as "Puritan foreshadowings" to the "tender years" doctrine that allowed mothers to have custody of their young children. But this doctrine would not be widely implemented until the early-nineteenth-century.[11]

The seriousness of Rogers's heterodox views surface in the court's decision to grant Elizabeth Griswold parental custody, but the details of the court proceedings went unrecorded. Colonial Connecticut courts lacked stenographers who could transcribe oral testimonies or legal arguments, and we can only surmise the words exchanged and emotions displayed. Obviously, much was at stake. The deep hurt Rogers felt from this decision is noted throughout his lifetime in his writings and repeated attempts to win back Elizabeth Griswold. As he always did during dark times, Rogers endeavored to find comfort and direction in the Scriptures. This ultimate source provided Rogers the fortitude to

---

[9] Rogers, Jr., *An Answer to a Book Lately Put Forth by Peter Pratt*, 36, 42.
[10] Caulkins, *History of New London*, 208.
[11] Cornelia Hughes Dayton, *Women before the Bar: Gender, Law, & Society in Connecticut, 1639-1789* (Chapel Hill: The University of North Carolina Press, 1995), 122-23.

press on. Despite this monumental setback, Rogers vowed to stay his dissenting course and eventually reconnect with his children. Thankfully for Rogers, he was able to establish a good relationship with both children when they reached adolescence.[12]

Legally both John, Jr. and Elizabeth, Jr. were required to live with their mother during their childhood years, but they both chose to live with their father when they were old enough to decide.[13] Elizabeth, Jr. resided with her father when she was about fourteen years of age and remained there until 1690 when she married Stephen Prentis of Bruen's Neck at nineteen years of age. John, Jr. attended his sister's wedding, and most likely reconnected with his father at this event. With his mother's permission, he was allowed to stay with his father as long as he pleased. When his stay extended too long, Elizabeth Griswold sent a constable to forcibly bring John, Jr. back to Lyme. It was just a matter of months before he broke free from his mother's grasp. John, Jr. insisted on living with his father and soon embraced Rogerene doctrine. John, Jr. believed he was called to be an itinerant preacher and hoped his father could help shape his future.[14]

What drew Rogers's children to him despite the opposition from their maternal relatives remains unknown. Rogers's interpersonal skills and character could account for his children's choices, and his relationship with Peter Pratt, Jr. could provide a window into his personality. Elizabeth Griswold remarried on August 5, 1679 to Peter Pratt of Lyme, and she gave birth to Peter, Jr. soon thereafter. As a young man Pratt, Jr. pursued the legal profession, which brought him to New London. While studying law in this port town, he reconnected with his half-brother, John Rogers, Jr., and soon found himself in the company of the elder Rogers. Within a short time after that, much to the horror of his mother, Pratt, Jr. embraced Rogerene doctrine. Rogers baptized Pratt, Jr. and took him under his wing as they both demonstrated against the Congregational laws and endured "fines, imprisonments, and public abuse" together for the Rogerene cause.[15]

After several years, Pratt, Jr. renounced his involvement with the

---

[12] Ibid., 5.
[13] Bolles and Williams, *The Rogerenes*, 141-42.
[14] Ibid., 159-73.
[15] Caulkins, *History of New London*, 208-9.

Rogerenes and authored a book titled *The Prey Taken From the Strong*. The book was obviously a defensive account of his dabbling with heterodox views and served as a biased account against Rogers. Still, as the title suggests, Rogers's personality was *strong*. If Pratt, Jr. viewed himself as the prey, he concluded that Rogers had the tenacity and scruples to catch religious seekers and persuade them to accept unorthodox views. Pratt, Jr. details in minutia his deep uncertainty about his relationship with the Almighty and how Rogers played an instrumental role in persuading him that the Rogerene path was the most scripturally accurate. Pratt, Jr. also recounts a time when a "certain Stranger who had been in a deep Concern about his Eternal Estate" came into conversation with Rogers, who "Preach'd to him." After this encounter, this stranger "soon became a Believer, and went on Rejoicing" as a follower of Rogers. Rogers's persuasive abilities appeared to be compelling.[16]

A bulk of Pratt, Jr.'s publication paints Rogers as cunning and duplicitous, and as a man who possessed the "Faculty to Relate [incidences] very Artfully in his *own Favour*." Further, he sympathized with fellow prey, such as his mother, who suffered Rogers's "Reproaches and Lies, at an execrable Rate (at the same time pretending the greatest Love)." According to Pratt, Jr., Rogers "Treated me with sufficient expressions of the tenderest Regard" when it was to his advantage only, and then proceeded to use him for Rogerene gain.[17] Since this book was published in 1725, three years after Rogers's death, his son, Rogers, Jr., came to his father's defense. He published a reply the following year titled *An Answer to a Book Lately Put Forth by Peter Pratt, Entituled, the Prey Taken from the Strong*. This book, along with Rogers, Jr.'s other publications attest to a close bond between father and son. Undoubtedly Rogers, Jr. heard unflattering remarks about his father from his mother and maternal grandparents as a child, but, still, he chose to embrace his father's sect when he became an adult. Rogers, Jr. wholeheartedly accepted Rogerene doctrine as truth and dedicated his life to further-

---

[16] Peter Pratt, Jr., *The Prey Taken from the Strong. Or, An historical account, of the recovery of one from the dangerous errors of Quakerism. An account of the principal articles of the Quaker faith, and especially of the New London Quakers the disciples of John Rogers. As also, a brief answer to John Rogers's boasting of his sufferings for his conscience, &c. With a word of advice to all who adhere to those doctrines* (New London: T. Green, 1725), 53

[17] Ibid., 2, 15, 55.

ing their beliefs. The only time there was contention between the two men was on the topic of marriage. Their contention was so sharp that it threatened to ruin their father-son relationship.

Trouble on the Home Front

After Rogers's divorce from Elizabeth Rowland was finalized, he found a new romantic interest. Rogers was fifty-two years old in 1699 when he paid for Mary Ransford's passage from England in exchange for indentured servitude. He was immediately drawn to her energy, and she accepted his advances wholeheartedly. Eventually she would become his common-law wife. While the couple celebrated their new love, a few family members were less than enthused, and Rogers, Jr. voiced the greatest objection. He vehemently resented Ransford's presence in his household and undoubtedly remembered that this servant girl replaced his mother.[18]

John Rogers, Jr.'s sentiments were not without provocation. Ransford was indeed an eccentric woman, and at times, difficult to understand. An ad circulating in New London in the early eighteenth century noted the hopeful arrest of a "Certain Woman poping up and Down" Connecticut by the "Name of Mary Rogers." By this time, Ransford had taken John Rogers's surname and regularly called herself Mary Rogers. The ad also noted that at other times she referred to herself as "Mary Remington, and some Times by other Names." The local courts deemed her an "evil" woman who caused "disorders of disturbance." Most disconcerting for New Londoners was that she "many Times Dresses in Mens Apparrell." Her name and physical description, that she was "a Woman of Midling Stature about 35 years," points to the fact that this sometimes cross-dressing disturber of the peace was indeed Mary Ransford. Moreover, she "hath two scars on the Back Part of her Neck Consealed by her apparel," which further authenticated Ransford's identity. She had gotten into many scrapes as a Rogerene and had been in physical altercations defending her husband's cause.[19]

Ransford's contentious disposition brought her to fisticuffs on

---
[18] Bolles and Williams, *The Rogerenes*, 196
[19] Connecticut State Library, Ecclesiastical Affairs, IV:111.

the home front as well. She and Rogers, Jr. let their tempers flare and unleashed their raw emotions on one another. Ransford ended up with "mark[s] upon her face" after she had used "wicked and notorious language" against Rogers, Jr. She called him "a sone of a Devil" and "sone of a whore, sone of a bitch."[20] Perhaps Ransford's words were spoken out of jealousy, and Rogers, Jr.'s harsh response was in defense of his mother's honor. Even at this phase of his life, Rogers's apparent love, if not obsession with, Elizabeth Griswold was known to everyone. It was no secret that Rogers still longed for his first wife even though she remarried twice. After Peter Pratt's death left her widowed on March 24, 1688, Elizabeth Griswold married Matthew Beckwith, Jr. from Lyme in 1691. She bore him one daughter, Griswold Beckwith, who would later become the wife of Eliakim Cooley, Jr. of Springfield. Court records indicate that Rogers harassed Elizabeth Griswold and Matthew Beckwith from time to time, and insisted that she was still rightfully his wife.[21]

Though Elizabeth Griswold was not a part of the Rogerene fold, it seems that her presence was palpably felt. Her son greatly resented Mary Ransford's replacement as the Rogers matriarch, and Ransford, in turn, became "so enraged as to threaten the life of" Rogers, Jr. "if God or man do not prevent it." The instability at home caused Rogers much anguish. Unable to control the domestic violence at home, the elder Rogers was forced to ask the court for assistance in quelling the disputes between his son and Ransford. Rogers, Jr. and Ransford were both fined ten shillings in 1700 for their inappropriate conduct.[22]

These were certainly difficult years for the Rogers family. For the first time, John Rogers, Jr. challenged his father's theology and morality and accused the elder Rogers of polygamy and hypocrisy. Rogers reasoned with his son by asking him "Did not God, in the olden times, allow two kinds of wives, both truly wives, yet one higher than the other?" Rogers maintained that Elizabeth Griswold was and always would be his first and most beloved wife, but argued a man could have a second wife without having annulled the first.[23]

---

[20] New London county Court Files, 1691-1702, Box 153, Connecticut State Archives, Connecticut State Library, Hartford, Connecticut, Rogers and Ransford, June 1700.
[21] Caulkins, *History of New London*, 209.
[22] Bolles and Williams, *The Rogerenes*, 201.
[23] Ibid., 198-99.

Rogers believed that remarrying, or in his case having a common-law wife, was acceptable, and this did not imply his acceptance of polygamy. His writings seem to note that many wives could be a part of a man's life but never must there be overlap. It appears that Rogers was referring to man's ability to remarry once his first and "honourable" wife was deceased or taken from him. Obviously in the case of a deceased wife a man was permitted to remarry, but this was not always the case for divorces in colonial times. Legislatures in certain states allowed for divorce but this did not automatically permit remarriage. For example, courts in New York and Virginia granted divorce on rare occasions but they were essentially separations that did not allow for remarriage. Only in the post-Revolutionary age was remarriage given as an option to those who were divorced regardless of reason.[24]

Interestingly, Rogers believed that morality had very little to do with polygamy. He explained it was "lawful" though perhaps "may not be expedient" for a man to have multiple wives at once. He justified his stance through the examples given by "Prophets and Servants of the Lord" who "had plurality of Wives." Citing Scripture, Rogers looked to Moses who had warned the Israelites "not to multiply Wives to themselves" and the Apostle Paul who cautioned his readers that "Bishops & Deacons (who were to be Leaders and Rulers in God's Church) were to be the Husbands of one Wife." Rogers rationalized these guidelines by arguing from a convenience standpoint rather than a moral one. Rogers believed a man with multiple wives would be too busy to adequately tend to the "care[s] of the Churches." Therefore, men "need to be free from the cares and cumbrances of more wives than one" in order to pursue an industrious and righteous life. He justified his union with Ransford by emphasizing his separation from Griswold; and true to his doctrine, Rogers never had more than one wife at a time.[25]

---

[24] Linda K. Kerber, *Women of the Republic: Intellect and Ideology in Revolutionary America* (Chapel Hill: University of North Carolina Press, 1980), 159.

[25] John Rogers, *A Mid-Night Cry from the Temple of God to the Ten Virgins Slumbering and Sleeping, Awake, Awake, Arise, and gird your Loyns, and trim your Lamps, for behold the Bridegroom cometh, go ye therefore out to meet him* (New London: Green, 1722), 155-68.

A Dichotomous Doctrine

While John Rogers, Jr. never accepted his father's reasons for acquiring a "second wife," the two men were mostly in agreement on women's roles in and outside of the house. Also, both men believed that foundational to the marriage unit were the civil laws that upheld this union, and the elder Rogers had much to say about this starting point. In fact, Rogers asserted that the reason for his "publishing this Treatise of *Marriage and Divorce*" was because "this Colony of Connecticut in New-England" rendered judgment on his divorce "contrary to the Rule of God[']s Word." This treatise, unsurprisingly, is buttressed with a variety of Old and New Testament passages on marriage. Starting with the first several chapters of Genesis, Ezekiel, and Malachi, Rogers referenced the Gospels and Epistles as well to reason why the marriage union was more than just a human contract. Using many verses from Mark 10, John 10, Romans 7, 1 Corinthians 7-11, and 2 Corinthians 11, Rogers contended that "the Woman taken out of the side of the Man, near his heart" were at one time "one flesh and bone." God created Eve *from* Adam to join them together in a "Bond of Union."[26]

Rogers believed no institution could separate the marriage covenant "without high Contempt against God's Authority." Going back to the Pentateuch, Rogers stated that "for the Lord, the God of Israel saith, that he hateth putting away [meaning divorce]." Rogers reiterated divorce is a "high Contempt aginst the Throne of God" for marriage "represents the Mystical Union between Christ and his Church, Ephes. 5:31, 32, and therefore it is written, *What God hath joyned together let no man put asunder*, Mark 10:9."

The only separation between family members sanctioned by Scripture, according to Rogers, was that between child and parent when the former was given in marriage. "God ordained a separation from Father and Mother, but a perpetual Union between a Man and his Wife." No doubt this line of reasoning was in direct response to Elizabeth Griswold's parents who pressed her to divorce Rogers. Further, Rogers ar-

---

[26] John Rogers, *An Epistle to the Churches of Christ call'd Quakers; And another epistle to the Seventh Day Baptists, with several Theological Essays* (New York: William Bradford, 1705), 83-88.

gued only husbands could initiate legal separation or divorce and only for the specific reason of fornication. Never should the husband, however, divorce his wife lightly since God warned his followers to "let none deal treacherously with the Wife of his Youth." Rogers deemed the husband as the wife's "Lord and Governour" and termed the wife as the husband's "peculiar Treasure" and "object of his greatest Delight."[27]

The husband was called to love and dote on his wife, but ultimately, she was his possession, according to Rogerene doctrine. As the one in subjection, Rogers argued, the wife "hath no power to put him away who is her Lord & Master." Under biblical laws, Rogers believed a wife was "subject" and "bound" to her husband, who "shall rule over her" as "long as she liveth." Should she abandon or divorce her husband, her sentence should be comparable to homicide. Rogers's justification for such a harsh penalty was taken from his rendition of the Scriptures: "by no means can [the wife] be loosed from this Bond of Union and Subjection to her Husband, without the breach of Wedlock, which in Scripture, the Punishment is equall'd with the punishment of Murder, Ezek. 16:38, *And I will judge thee as Women that break Wedlock and shed Blood are judged.*"[28]

Rogers believed Congregational laws were too liberal for permitting divorce for reasons other than fornication. Rogers stated fornication was distinct from adultery because it was "an act done before Marriage" rather than during.[29] In a case where a woman married a man under false pretense of being a virgin, thereby being a fornicator, Rogers believed divorce should be granted. The man upon discovering "he is cheated" and she was not a "Virgin or Chaste Woman when he hath taken her," would not be obligated to stay in such a marriage because the union was predicated upon fraudulent claims. As God is "not the Author of deceit," Rogers believed a man should rightfully be granted a divorce in such cases. Adultery was a different matter altogether. If a man caught his wife in the act of marital infidelity, he had no right to divorce or separation according to Rogerene directives.[30]

---

[27] Ibid., 159-73.
[28] Ibid., 83-88.
[29] Rogers, *A Mid-Night Cry from the Temple of God*, 151-53.
[30] Rogers, *An Epistle to the Churches of Christ call'd Quakers*, 86-88.

Referring to his own parents' divorce, John Rogers, Jr. stated that the General Court "granted *John Rogers's* Wife a Bill of Divorce, without giving any reason why they did it, which I suppose to be a Precedent not to be Parallel in the Kingdom of *England*."[31] Rogers, Jr. was essentially stating that the courts condoned a no-fault divorce, which was unheard of in colonial times. Of course this was not the case, but still, Rogers, Jr. decried Congregational courts as being too liberal and backslidden compared to the marital laws of the Old World. Divorce was granted in colonial courts on a variety of charges, including adultery, desertion, impotence, and absence for a specified length of time.[32] Rogerenes believed that a more stringent system of familial governance was necessary in the colonies and pushed to curb women's access to divorce.

Before the Revolution, each colony maintained its own divorce laws and Connecticut's were the most liberal of all. Comparatively, South Carolina did not allow divorce as a legal option, and New York and Virginian laws treated divorce as an ecclesiastical rather than legal matter and only scarcely allowed for it. New England was a rarity in that marriage was viewed as a civil contract which could be broken if certain terms were not met. Out of the New England territories, Connecticut's divorce statutes were the laxest with "options unavailable elsewhere in the British Empire."[33] Looking at Connecticut's court records, Henry S. Cohn concludes that divorce was largely regarded as a customary option in colonial times.[34]

Feeling betrayed by the laws of Connecticut, Rogers vowed never to hold sacred the union of marriage as prescribed by Congregational governance. Instead, Rogers vowed to uphold the sanctity of marriage his own way. Rogers refused to marry Ransford in the conventional sense, but his refusal to legalize their union had little to do with his commitment to her as a monogamous partner. Rogers resolved never to trust in or abide by Congregational practices in matrimony after his divorce

---

[31] Rogers, Jr., *An Answer to a Book Lately Put Forth by Peter Pratt*, 37.
[32] Edmund Morgan, *The Puritan Family: Religion and Domestic Relations in Seventeenth-Century New England* (New York: Harper & Row, 1944), 35-37.
[33] Kerber, *Women of the Republic*, 159-161.
[34] Henry S. Cohn, "Connecticut's Divorce Mechanism: 1636-1969," *American Journal of Legal History*, XLIV (1970): 35-54.

from Griswold. Upon his own research, Rogers concluded "The holy Scriptures prescribes no Ceremonies in Marriage" but "it gives us an account of how *Boaz* gave public notice of his Marriage with *Ruth*." Believing that a simple public notice was sufficient to seal the bonds of marriage, Rogers escorted Ransford through the streets of New London and orally pronounced their wedding sometime between 1699 and 1700.[35] The author Bolles notes that their marriage was "well-authenticated" as Rogers informed Governor Fitz-John Winthrop of his marriage to Ransford, and the Governor politely wished them much joy.[36] Such a response from the governor was never authenticated, nor does it seem probable in light of ensuing legal repercussions that Rogers and Ransford faced for their unsanctioned union according to New London law.

When Judge Wetherell, a local justice, offered to marry them, Rogers refused and continued on with his pronouncement. Rogers and Ransford were embroiled in a host of legal charges stemming from their unlawful marital relations that resulted in two children being born out of wedlock. The first was a son named Gershom, and the second was a daughter named after her mother, Mary. Obviously, the New London courts did not honor Rogers's self-proclaimed union to Ransford, and they "suffered Persecution for the First [child] according to law" and were "Examined by Authorit[ies]" for conceiving their second child out of wedlock. In June 1700, the County Court fined Mary Ransford forty shillings for bearing an illegitimate child. Rogers, on behalf of Ransford and himself, appealed to the Superior Court, and the matter was dropped on technical grounds. The County Court had failed to provide "due forms of law" and the initial fine was considered "invalid."[37]

After Rogers fathered a second child with Ransford, both were summonsed before the court for this unlawful act. Before taking the stand, Rogers had solemnly warned Ransford not to take an oath, but she broke under the pressures exerted by the magistrates. Under oath, she declared that John Rogers was indeed the father of her purported

---

[35] Bolles and Williams, *The Rogerenes*, 198-200; Rogers, *A Mid-Night Cry from the Temple of God*, 174-75.
[36] Ibid., 198-99.
[37] Ibid., 200-201, 265.

bastard children. There seems to be ambiguity regarding what the oath entailed. It appears that the oath was one where if Ransford complied, she would esteem her marriage to Rogers as unlawful and her children illegitimate. It is unclear whether Rogers's anger toward Ransford was due to the physical act of taking an oath or to the specific indications of the oath itself. Regardless, his umbrage towards her was so great that "upon some Disgust, put [Ransford] away." Ransford left New London in 1703 and left her children behind.[38]

Interestingly, the births of these two illegitimate children fell during the "transitional years" of 1690-1740. During this phase, Connecticut witnessed an increasingly lax standard for unmarried women to remain silent about the father of their children and for unmarried men to evade prosecution for fornication. The fact that the courts refused to overlook either births shows that for obvious reasons the Rogerenes were under the watchful eye of the government. After failing to properly indict Rogers and Ransford for the birth of their first child, the courts were ready when their second child was born. At this point, the courts had to intervene to stop Rogers's brazen law breaking, and their intervention was effective. After two children and three years with John Rogers, Ransford left New London and eventually married legally Robert Jones from Block Island in 1710. In 1714, Rogers married Sarah Coles, a widowed Quaker from Oyster Bay, Long Island, and the two married legally within the jurisdiction of Rhode Island. No familial or legal problems arose from Rogers's marriage with Coles. Little is recorded of Oyster, except that she was a "zealous religious co-worker with her husband" and possessed an "attractive personality."[39]

Rogers's "complex marital history" seems to fit his convoluted notions on marriage and the roles of husband and wife.[40] And although Rogers accused the Congregationalists of giving wives too much power in society, his ideas on women in general were more in line with traditional sectarian positions. Women with an independent streak, such as

---

[38] Bolles and Williams, *The Rogerenes*, 202-4; Frances Manwaring Caulkins, *History of New London, Connecticut: From the First Survey of the Coast in 1612, to 1860* (New London: H.D. Utley, 1895), 217; Pratt, *The Prey Taken from the Strong*, 58-61.
[39] Bolles and Williams, T*he Rogerenes*, 241; Caulkins, *History of New London*, 218.
[40] John L. Brooke, *The Refiner's Fire: The Make of Mormon Cosmology, 1644-1844* (Cambridge: Cambridge University Press, 1994), 85.

Ransford, would naturally be drawn away from the Congregational fold. In general, dissenting groups offered "a measure of personal judgment" that afforded women more autonomy. For example, "Catholics offered an alternative to marriage, Baptists a choice of voluntary submission as adults, Quakers a more participatory role, and Anglicans an ability to reclaim the self through works." Further, of all the non-Congregational groups, the Quakers alone "even approached equality." Quaker women were allowed to vote on a host of topics and contribute during their regular meetings. The Rogerenes, like the Quakers, allowed women a greater voice in day-to-day affairs than their Puritan counterparts, and Ransford undoubtedly found liberating the opportunity to actively participate as demonstrator and dissenter.[41] Interestingly, Ransford apparently inspired succeeding generation of Rogerenes to follow a dissenting path, and Ransford Rogers, a great-nephew of John Rogers, was named after this "second wife" and indeed charted an unconventional path through divination and magic.[42]

There are a host of testimonies where Rogerene women fought alongside their men for their doctrinal cause. For example, Mary Ransford often took part in Rogerene demonstrations, but they were at the guidance and consent of Rogers. She was an extremely feisty woman who was arraigned in court for throwing "scalding water out of the window upon the head of the constable who came to collect their minister's rate." Also, she joined Rogers in 1693 in battering a constable as he was taking away a barrel of beef in lieu of unpaid minister's rates. Rogers heartily consented to such actions so long as they were under his management. Other Rogerene women, such as Bathshua Fox, wife of Rogerene Samuel Fox, often went to the Congregational meetinghouse to announce publicly that she had been doing "servile work" on the Sabbath. These among many other Rogerene women participated in dissenting activities alongside and with the approval of Rogerene men.[43]

Despite the fact that Rogerene women were active in demonstrating against Congregationalists alongside their men, they were under the

---

[41] Elaine Forman Crane, *Ebb Tide in New England: Women, Seaports, and Social Change, 1630-1800* (Boston: Northeastern University Press, 1998), 59, 73.
[42] Ibid., 53.
[43] Caulkins, *History of New London*, 212, 216.

careful supervision of their husbands or male counterparts. Though it may seem Rogerene women were in visible roles outside the home, as orators, teachers, and demonstrators, they were mostly under the direction of their male leaders. The watchful governance over sectarian women, however, was a normal practice for religious dissenters in colonial times. Though sectarians were progressive in allowing women to take on more religious responsibilities than the Standing Order, they were still products of their patriarchal traditions. Like other sectarians, such as Quakers and Baptists, Rogerenes afforded more share of church governance than did the Congregationalists, but they were still very much rooted in a male-dominated leadership.[44]

As in other aspects of Rogerene theology, traditional beliefs undercut the dissenting elements of their doctrine. In particular, a personal topic like marriage has a way of reiterating deeply held traditions. While he was fascinated by and adopted many sectarian tenets, Rogers could not break away from his core indoctrination of Congregationalism. Rogerene theology on women is the most apt illustration of this dueling inner-self. In fact, a close survey of Rogerene doctrine on matters concerning women indicates that John Rogers was even more stringent than were the Congregationalists. Rogers accused Congregationalists of granting women too much power in matters of marital relations and believed the New England laws were too lenient in their allowance for divorce. As sectarians, Rogerenes believed that both men and women should be able to publicly speak in meetings and women who were "gifted by the Spirit" should be teachers.[45] Such latitude, however, was harshly curtailed when it came to women's roles in marriages and in the home.

A Dead End

Whether the topic was the role of women or the road to salvation, Rogerene doctrine was well published and publicized, and Rogers spent an inordinate amount of time and parchment expositing his Scriptural interpretations on these matters. Unfortunately for the Rogerenes, their ideals were not accepted as popular

---
[44] Crane, *Ebb Tide in New England*, 73.
[45] Ellen Starr Brinton, "The Rogerenes" *New England Quarterly* 16, no. 1 (1943): 3-19.

creed in colonial New London. The failure of the Rogerenes to provide a viable theological alternative to Congregationalism was the main reason for their downfall as indicated through a detailed survey of their ideals. While Quakers and Sabbatarians thought Rogerenes were too entrenched in Congregational thought for their liking, the Standing Order disagreed and accused them of blasphemy for incorporating radical sectarian principles. Rogers believed that these reprimands only validated his quest for religious authenticity. The Standing Order, in Rogers's eye, was horribly corrupt. Their wrongful interpretation of Scripture was the main bone of contention. Rogers was every bit as intolerant as the Puritans; and his main concern was not of religious freedom but of religious purity.

Although Rogers did not leave behind personal, diary-like reflections, he did pen many books and treatises that chronicle his devolvement from model citizen to outcast. Just as one's outside persona is not an accurate reflection of the private man, one's public writings are not necessarily indicative of one's inner thoughts. Still, historians can piece together through Rogers's writings a metamorphosis of theology and character. Rogers's transformation had ripple effects that originated with his family and flowed into religious and civic affairs in profound ways. Rogers's deflection from Congregationalism caused a venerated family to redefine social privilege, resulted in a landmark divorce case to be etched into American history, and created the first indigenous sect in the colonies. These are certainly noteworthy events.

John Rogers lived a long and full life, dedicated to following his conscience and the Scriptures. His writings and actions prove that he was a man committed to individual convictions that were deeply steeped in biblical precepts. Toward the latter years of his life, he was able to sum up his core beliefs in two publications. In *The Book of the Revelation of Jesus Christ* and *John Rogers a Servant of Jesus Christ*, Rogers detailed the importance of sharing one's faith with others. The imparting of one's views may cause a stir or be met with resistance, but Rogers was convinced that it was his duty to share his revelations with others no matter the cost. Rogers, once again, turned to the Scriptures and used biblical examples, such as Jesus and the apostles, as perfect symbols of religious resoluteness. And eventually, like these martyrs,

Rogers's persistence cost him his life.

Rogers went to Boston to publish more of his doctrine in October 1721 but came back with a fever. A smallpox epidemic raged in Boston but he visited anyway. Rogers had been in the presence of those infected with smallpox before, but he had luckily remained healthy. Unfortunately for Rogers, this time he contracted the disease and fell ill. After suffering through a high fever and being quarantined in his home, John Rogers died on Mamacock farm on October 17, 1721 at the age of seventy-three. Upon his death, the inventory of Rogers's worth was tallied; his estate was valued at £410 and included several chests filled with his own books, seven Bibles and Powell's and Clarke's concordances.[46] Incidentally, Rogers's death fell on the same day as his and Elizabeth Griswold's anniversary day.[47]

---

[46] Bolles and Williams, *The Rogerenes*, 264; Vavasor Powell, *A New and Useful Concordance to the Holy Bible. Whereunto is added, the chief acceptations & various significations contained in the Old and New Testament. Also a collection of those Scripture-prophesies which relate to the call of the Jews* (London: R. Clark, 1671). Samuel Clark, *A Brief concordance to the Holy Bible, of the most usual and useful places which one may have occasion to seek for in a new method* (London: T. Parkhurst, 1696).
[47] Caulkins, *History of New London*, 221.

SOLA SCRIPTURA

Conclusion

Soon after the death of their patriarch and founder, the Rogerenes suffered further loss as John Rogers III died on November 6, 1721 at twenty-one years of age, and Bathsheba Rogers, cousin and wife of John Rogers, Jr., died on November 13, 1721. They also died from smallpox.[1] John Rogers, Jr.'s loss of his father, son, and wife must have been devastating. His wife had been the daughter of John Rogers's sister of the same name and known as Rogers's "favorite niece."[2] The couple had lived at Mamacock Farm in New London, and Bathsheba Rogers had given birth to eighteen children, who were all raised as "sturdy Rogerenes."[3] Bathsheba Rogers had assumed the roles of dutiful wife and mother at home and gutsy demonstrator in public, and she was sorely missed.

Despite his grief, John Rogers, Jr. vowed to press on. He earned a reputation as "Naturally a Man as Manly, Wise, Facetious, and Generous, perhaps as one amongst a Thousand" and a great conversationalist.[4] He immediately assumed the Rogerene leadership in 1721 upon his father's death and fought to keep their doctrines alive. He encouraged the Rogerenes to continue their various protests and to disseminate their doctrine as widely as possible. John Bolles and John Waterhouse also stepped up into positions of leadership, assuming ministerial roles. The second-generation Rogerenes, however, failed to expand upon their founder's vision or recapture a zeal for the Scriptures that had burned brightly in the elder Rogers. After their founder's death, the Rogerenes only repeated the same demonstrations that had grown hackneyed by the late 1720s.

---

[1] Frances Manwaring Caulkins, *History of New London, Connecticut: From the First Survey of the Coast in 1612, to 1860* (New London: H.D. Utley, 1895), 221.
[2] John R. Bolles and Anna B. Williams, *The Rogerenes: Some Hitherto Unpublished Annals Belonging to the Colonial History of Connecticut* (Boston: Stanhope Press, 1904), 200.
[3] Caulkins, *History of New London*, 209.
[4] Peter Pratt, Jr., *The Prey Taken from the Strong. Or, An historical account, of the recovery of one from the dangerous errors of Quakerism. An account of the principal articles of the Quaker faith, and especially of the New London Quakers the disciples of John Rogers. As also, a brief answer to John Rogers's boasting of his sufferings for his conscience, &c. With a word of advice to all who adhere to those doctrines* (New London: T. Green, 1725), 1, 11.

The Rogerenes became increasingly quiet as the years wore on. They practiced their faith, but in a calm and deferential manner that was unknown in earlier years. Rogerene leaders continued to publish books in defense of their doctrines and to hold their own meetings. But there was very little Rogerene activity in the ensuing thirty years, and a palpable silence was felt during the Great Awakening. After John Rogers, Jr.'s death in 1753, John Rogers IV, along with Samuel Whipple and John Bolles, Jr., kept the movement alive. These men revived their founder's vision by reprinting Rogers's books and putting his theories into practice.

There was a new wave of persecution against the Rogerenes in 1760 led by the Reverend Mather Byles, Jr., pastor of the Congregational Church in New London. Persecution became especially intense during the two years between 1764 and 1766. The central contention once again pointed to issues surrounding the Sabbath. Demonstrations against the Sabbath in the latter years resembled the archetype modeled by Rogers: Rogerene women sewed and knitted during service times, and men refused to remove their broad-brimmed beaver hats during Congregational meetings.

Just as Rogers harnessed his energies to beleaguer Gurdon Saltonstall, the latter-day Rogerenes set their sights on Byles, whom they targeted in their protests against Congregational standards. They disturbed his preaching at the New London meetinghouse on Sundays and congregated in front of his house on weekdays as a gesture of silent protest. Historian Ellen Brinton notes that such actions would be tantamount to picketing in our current day. After months of such activity, Byles appeared to get "more and more nervous" until, suddenly, he resigned his post in New London for another one in Boston.[5]

The years preceding the American Revolution brought times of upheaval. New ideas circulated and competed against old ones, and terms such as "tyranny" and "liberty" dominated everyday discussions. The Rogerenes largely disbanded by the end of the American Revolution but were contributors in the making of the American consciousness. The third generation visibly put into practice Rogers's ideals that led to individualistic acts. For example, the Bolles household believed

---

[5] Ellen Starr Brinton, "The Rogerenes," *New England Quarterly* 16, no. 1 (1943): 12.

that matters of conscience were of utmost importance and applied this concept to the realm of slavery. John Bolles, Jr. and other Rogerene leaders were convinced that spiritual equality must equal racial equality. Bolles, Jr. often preached on the evils of slavery and legally freed his own slaves. Other Rogerenes likewise followed their own convictions, which led them to fight for fair economic dealings with Native Americans. Among the third generation sectarians, individual convictions led the Rogerenes to fight for the disenfranchised.

Third generation Rogerenes, however, had lost sight of their founder's original premise. While both Rogers and his third generation followers wanted to create a state based on individual convictions, their reasons were radically different. As the brewing revolution intensified, John Rogers IV and Samuel Whipple were among the clamoring voices that emphasized the importance of following one's conscience. While it seemed that John Rogers had sung the same tune nearly a century prior, in reality, such was not the case. When Rogers cried out for autonomy of conscience, his pronouncement came from an intense reading of Scripture and a zealous desire to please the Almighty. Such pietistic impulses were foreign to third generation Rogerenes.

These succeeding generations failed to grasp that Rogers had an Augustinian strain of purity in mind when he founded his sect. This type of holy living had been embedded within the mindset of the first generation Congregationalists, and Rogers had aimed for its revival. Rogers's vision of a city on a hill differed in many ways from Puritan notions, but the desire for greater spirituality was foundational to both. Unfortunately for Rogers, no generation of Puritans deemed his religious views as a serious alternative. If Rogerene doctrine was anathema to his contemporaries, then these precepts appeared dated and too mystical to those who were fast becoming Yankees. Rogerene doctrine could not appeal to the religious sentiments of second and third generation Congregationalists, who were increasingly relying on external conformity as a measure of virtue.

Congregationalists of any generation did not deal kindly with religious sectarians. The reasons for stamping out dissent changed from generation to generation, but protecting the Standing Order remained constant. First generation Congregationalists focused on safeguarding ideals related to holiness and salvation because outward obedience was not the central concern. For example, the Antinomian crisis principally revolved around theological matters pertaining to preparation. Of course there were external issues such as the role of women and creating divisions amongst townspeople; and historians have cited the jealousy of Congregational preachers as a partial motive behind the Hutchinson trial. But as Perry Miller points out, Hutchinson's main problem was that she believed that no amount of preparation could indeed prepare one for salvation. In essence, she proclaimed that God "rapes our souls" through immediate revelation.[6]

The Antinomian crisis was chiefly about the theology of preparation, rather than an external focus on compulsory adherence. When Rogers contended with Congregationalists, the emphasis was reversed. The Congregationalists of Rogers's generation were concerned with outer compliance rather than doctrinal matters. These Congregationalists were content with monopolizing ideals that would retain social conformity because piety seemed like an elusive goal.

Puritans had begun to act less and less Puritanical by the rise of the Rogerenes. The Rogerenes were birthed at a time when Congregational leaders were no longer unified in their own religious identities, which made outward compliance all the more important. Eighteenth-century Congregationalists were increasingly concerned with social conformity rather than theological justifications for an outward manifestation. In fact, by the late-seventeenth century Puritans were in danger of becoming the civil man whom the preachers had warned against.[7] They justified this emphasis by highlighting the importance of the state covenant. Puritans ceased being Puritans around this time, because they cared less about why the townspeople came to the meetinghouse than that they did.

---

[6] Perry Miller, *The New England Mind: From Colony to Province* (Cambridge: Harvard University Press, 1953), 57-59.

[7] The following excerpt by Edmund Morgan is the best illustration of the civil man: "There was a type of man whom the Puritans never tired of denouncing. He was a good citizen, a man who obeyed the laws, carried out his social obligations, never injured others. The Puritans called him a 'civil man,' and admitted that he was 'outwardly just, temperate, chaste, careful to follow his worldly businesse, will not hurt so much as his neighbours dog, payes every man his owne, and lives to his owne; no drunkard, adulterer, or quareller; loves to live peaceably and quietly among his neighbours.' This man, this paragon of social virtue, the Puritans said, was on his way to Hell, and their preachers continually reminded him of it." Edmund Morgan, *The Puritan Family: Religion and Domestic Relations in Seventeenth-Century New England* (New York: Harper & Row, 1944), 1. Inner quote by Thomas Hooker, *The Christian Two Chiefe Lessons* (London: n.p., 1640), 213.

As Perry Miller points out, Congregational ministers would have been satisfied with pews packed with hypocrites, so long as they acted as told.[8]

Rogers launched theological battles in print against the Congregationalists, who were in no mood for such debates. There were plenty of theological arguments amongst themselves, with the Matherses and Solomon Stoddard at odds about communion and other such traditional and nontraditional Congregationalists who differed on various tenets. They certainly did not need dissenters like Rogers to exacerbate the situation by pointing out their inconsistencies with one another and accusing them of deviating from their forebears. Ironically, it appeared that Rogers better understood that New England was founded upon ideals that exceeded merely upright behavior. Rogers preached that motives outweighed actions and God's judgment superseded man's.

Congregationalists in New London did their best to enforce conformity, but they understood that the city port created a heterogeneous environment. They could not expect the same level of compliance and orthodoxy in New London as they did in Hartford or New Haven. And this was obviously an advantage for religious dissenters who desired to worship freely. There were disadvantages, however, to a religiously mixed atmosphere for dissenters who were unsatisfied with mere tolerance. In a way, the laxer attitude toward religious observances in a port town contributed to Rogers's difficulties. He wanted to spread a vital Christianity that was no longer fashionable at the turn of the eighteenth century. The rise of secularization was especially apparent in places like New London.

Rogers spent his entire adult life proselytizing in an area where there was growing secularism, emotionalism, or Arminianism, but certainly not pietism. There were those who cared very little for religious matters, and these secularists turned a deaf ear to Rogers's message of piety. Likewise, emotionalists cared little for Rogerene doctrine since they were already snugly situated in their own faiths (mostly as Quakers and Sabbatarians). Congregationalists, with their presbyteries and emphasis on works, were becoming more Arminian in various ways, and they, of all people, refused to listen to Rogers.

In a way, Rogers preached against declension when he articulated his desire for a fervent holiness. But if the Matherses and other

---
[8] Miller, *The New England Mind: From Colony to Province*, 77-78.

Congregational leaders could not stop the onslaught of secularization, Rogers certainly had no chance. Perhaps Rogers would have made more progress if he had deviated from the orthodoxy towards a material rather than a spiritual bent. For example, had he followed the lead of Solomon Stoddard, he might have garnered more support. Although Stoddard was outside the Cambridge Association, he dominated the Connecticut Valley by lowering standards for baptism and for partaking in the Lord's Supper. It appeared that New Englanders were flocking to congregations that reduced requirements for religious ordinances.

A telltale sign of the growing worldliness is the amicable exchanges between the Congregationalists, Rogerenes, and other sectarian groups. Romantic liaisons, business exchanges, and social interactions between people of differing faiths were not a rarity by the late seventeenth century. Religion was certainly not the only determinant in social or personal decisions. And sometimes, it was not even a part of the equation. Of course religious affiliations were an important aspect of one's identity but so were other factors, such as wealth, vocation, and personal interests. By the start of the eighteenth century, people were beginning to be judged by standards apart from religious association, much less on matters pertaining to piety or divine election.

Rogers spent a significant amount of time meeting with New Londoners of varied faiths and proved that it was possible to disagree about theological matters in a civilized fashion. Rogers and other sectarians attempted to reprove one another but their words and tone mostly remained respectful and, at times, friendly and inviting. The interacting of different faiths did have evangelism at its core, but the participants also experienced camaraderie and intellectual stimulation. These exchanges forced Rogers to search the Scriptures all the more diligently and provide a sound defense for his beliefs.

Rogers sternly warned his fellow Rogerenes to abstain from "fellowship" with those of different beliefs, but he also spent much time reaching out to and defending those of non-Rogerene persuasion. This apparent contradiction was reconciled under the Rogerene understanding of denominationalism and its implications upon civic and religious life. Rogers understood that they were varied faiths in New England with differing opinions on a host of canonical issues. Dissimilarities, however, should not bar interaction with one another. In fact, differences of opinion, when aired and shared in a civilized manner, can often lead to a greater realization of truth.

In many instances Rogers's attitude toward the Quakers was no different than his approach toward his fellow Rogerenes. He regarded individual Quaker societies as legitimate "Churches of Christ" and addressed their leaders by proper titles, such as "Elders." He extended "Grace and Peace" to the Quakers, as if they were all from "one flock." At one point, Rogers even called the Society of Friends "Beloved in the Lord" and as God's instruments to bring truth to those seeped in darkness.[9]

Surprisingly, Rogers even went as far as legitimizing their proper relationship with God, as he acknowledged "the blessed day of the Lords appearing unto you, when [He] first illuminated you." The referenced date of "illuminat[ion]" is unknown, but what is certain is Rogers's assurance that Christ did reveal himself to the Society of Friends. Rogers admitted that "it greatly affects [his] heart" when he considers upon this fortunate event. The result of God's unveiling of Himself to the Quakers was their willingness to fight for the truth. Rogers commended them for enduring "a great fight of Affliction" against the Congregationalists as he had done to his own followers. Most likely referring to Marmaduke Stevenson and William Robinson who were executed by the Congregationalists, Rogers assured the Society of Friends that "being slain for the Word of God" was a "great blessing."[10]

Rogers's interactions with Congregationalists were not always adversative or combative either. Despite the stringent enforcement of Congregational laws, Rogers managed to immerse himself into New London life as a productive and, at times, accepted citizen. The rights-based interpretation of sectarian advancement has caused historians to overlook peaceful interactions between Rogers and Congregationalists. Their amicable exchanges are important etches into the broader canvas of religious life in colonial New London.

Sectarians have often been characterized as exclusionary people who did not know or experience life outside of their tightly-knit, faith-based communities. A study of the Rogerenes, however, disproves the

---
[9] Ibid.
[10] Ibid.

notion that religious dissenters were principally outside the realm of accepted society and did not partake in town activities apart from religious pursuits. Rogerenes were active citizens in New London, people integrally a part of town affairs. The Rogerenes had extensive contact with those outside of their faith who resided in New London and in surrounding colonies.

For example, James Rogers had been a prominent member in New London society since its founding, and even after his Rogerene conversion he was regarded as a contributing member of society. Their townsmen also viewed his children, including John Rogers, as industrious and capable people. James Rogers often entertained Congregationalists after his Rogerene conversion. And so long as he ran the bakery in town, he continued to be generous with his bread as well as his money. He contributed his resources to benefit New London in tangible ways, such as feeding the needy and contributing monetarily to beautify the roads. When James Rogers died in February 1687, he was still an active member of the Congregational church. No account of his secession from Bradstreet's church in New London remains.[11]

Rogerenes married, traded with, and socialized with those outside of their religious belief.[12] Such interactions must have been necessary because there were never more than two-hundred Rogerenes at a given time. John Rogers personally contributed as a citizen of New London, and, apart from his demonstrations, was considered a worthy inhabitant. Historian Francis Caulkins notes that Rogers "was never disfranchised." When out of prison he was always ready with his vote" and was often chosen to some town office, such as sealer of leather, or surveyor of highways.[13] Although these were not high posts, still, Rogers proved to be deemed a responsible member of society. This was also true for other sectarians. For example, Jonathan Chu notes throughout his book the various public offices Quakers held in New England towns.[14]

---

[11] Caulkins, *History of New London*, 29, 207.

[12] There is a vague reference in Rogers's writing that Congregationalists might have taught that "no man must buy or sell" to those who refuse to take part in Congregational beliefs. This was a part of Rogers's exposition on Revelation and is more likely his understanding of the biblical reference to the "mark of the beast" than the Congregationalists' insistence on excluding commercial activities to those outside of their beliefs. (Rogers, John Rogers, *A Servant of Jesus Christ*, 29-30).

[13] Caulkins, *History of New London*, 216.

[14] Jonathan M. Chu, *Neighbors, Friends, or Madmen: The Puritan Adjustment to Quakerism in Seven-*

When they acted lawfully and in compliance with church rules, they were accepted as fellow citizens in New London. Rogerenes had regular and amicable contact with fellow sectarians, as well as with Congregationalists in their midst. For example, John Rogers preached at Thomas Young's house on Saturday, February 24, 1694. Young was a wealthy Congregationalist who had converted to a Rogerene and baptized at the hands of Rogers on November 6, 1692. Among the attendees at Young's house that day were Gurdon Saltonstall, John Christophers, and Daniel Wetherell, who listened attentively to Rogers's teaching. Afterward, the men ensued in an amicable exchange and talked about theological matters. Although Rogers was arrested the following day, it was not for the differences in theology but, rather, that he worked on the Sunday Sabbath.[15]

At such meetings, there were important New London officials such as Saltonstall and Christophers, but also often a "large numbers gathered to listen to this discourse." This indicates that many Congregationalists were exposed to Rogerene faith. No mention of charges, imprisonments, or fines is shown in New London town records for conducting such sessions. The possibility of sharing sectarian faiths to Congregational audiences in an acceptable fashion is recognized through John Rogers's interaction with the Standing Order.

Many townspeople, who were mainstream, run-of-the-mill Congregationalists, also interacted with Rogerenes in neighborly ways. After Rogers refused to pay a fine for contempt of court in September 1711, he was placed in a cold jail cell without any heat. The conditions were inhumane and purposefully concocted to cause Rogers's acquiescence. John Rogers, Jr. alerted the townspeople to this fact by running through town and conveying the situation. Upon hearing the news, the townspeople rose up and demanded Rogers be released before he died of the cold.

The amicable exchanges between Rogerenes and Congregationalists have largely escaped the notice of historians because they are buried underneath a mountain of legal sanctions and church censures. Congregationalist authorities, both civil and religious, undoubtedly found

---

teenth-Century Massachusetts Bay (Westport: Greenwood Press, 1985), 27.
[15] Bolles and Williams, *The Rogerenes*, 67-69, 176-79.

the Rogerenes troublesome, but this does not mean that their sentiments were as such at all times. Also, the romantic liaisons and friendships that were born between Rogerenes and Congregationalists were often stronger sentiments that overrode religious convictions. Just as proselytizing trumped unified demonstrations in sectarian interactions, visceral elements prevailed over religious differences when Rogerenes intermingled with Congregationalists.

A number of marriages occurred between Rogerenes and Congregationalists, indicating that differences in faith did not bar a deeper connection within New Londoners. One way of attracting converts to the Rogerene faith was through marriage. In 1684, Samuel Beebe, Jr., the eldest son of one of the most "substantial citizens" in New London, met the acquaintance of Elizabeth Rogers, sister of John Rogers. Beebe courted Elizabeth Rogers despite the fact that she was an active Rogerene member and he was part of the Congregational fold. The two married in 1684, and, thereafter, there appeared the slow "conforming to the [Rogerene] faith" by Beebe. A similar event is noted in 1693 when Samuel Fox, a member of the Congregational church in New London and one of the most prosperous businessmen in town, married Bathsheba Smith, a Rogerene, and then adopted her faith.[16]

Frequent interactions between people of differing faiths indicate that religion was not the only determinant in social or personal decisions. Religious identity did not prohibit people from making connections with those of divergent beliefs. While religion was a dominant part of colonial culture and certainly on the minds of many colonists, it appears to have been intermingled with other, more primal, elements such as love, desire, and curiosity. Moreover, not everyone necessarily had an abiding interest in religion and needed to be defined by matters of faith. Samuel Rogers was married to a woman from a prominent Congregational family in New London. He seemed rather lacking in interest in religious affairs in general and never cared too deeply about the Rogerene or Congregational faiths. He devoted most of his time to the bakery business he had inherited. He also spent much time in uncharted areas, especially current-day Montville, and even befriended nearby Native Americans. Legend has it that Samuel was a "great favorite" of

---
[16] Ibid., 157, 173.

the Mohegan chief, Owaneco, son of Uncas.[17]

New London was a place where sectarians found a refuge of sorts in a strictly Congregational colony. Weak political and spiritual leadership, and the wealth and social connections of Rogerene leaders all contributed to sectarian advances in New London. This was certainly a place ripe for dissent, and John Rogers made the most of his opportunities. Rogers's defection from Congregationalism and adherence to Sabbatarianism was one example of how a New Londoner could question the legitimacy of Puritanism; and the creation of his own sect shows the limits that New Londoners could test and push in terms of religious expression and experimentation. This small but important sect shows the religious and civic boundaries that New Londoners faced on a day-to-day basis and how forcefully citizens could push back with and without reprisal.

And while Rogers decried the loss of piety, he made the most of his commercial opportunities. Rogers was a man devoted to a holy life, but he was also a shrewd businessman who made the most of the burgeoning economy. As the son of a prominent New Londoner, he was an important player in local and long-distance trade and was adept in the commercial and legal arenas. Rogers's engagement in overseas trade allowed him to meet people of varied religious persuasions, which ultimately gave rise to his unique theology. Interactions with European merchants shaped Rogers's theology and ideals regarding many key elements that comprised core Rogerene doctrine. Along with John Rogers, other leading Rogerenes were also wealthy New London inhabitants who were actively engaged in the transatlantic trade.

In both religious and legal affairs Rogers leveraged his wealth and status to further his sectarian causes. His father and many of his siblings joined the Rogerene movement, which meant that the Rogerses lent their wealth and social standing to this sectarian cause. And others who had descended from notable New London families, such as John Culver, Samuel Beeby, and John Bolles, assumed leadership positions within the Rogerene ranks. Due to his wealth, Rogers was able to intimidate Congregational leaders. For example, he threatened to launch international lawsuits and appeal to the Crown. There was no faster ave-

---
[17] Ibid., 166.

nue to stop Congregational harassment than to cite English laws. Rogers often invoked the 1689 Toleration Act as defense against compulsory tithing or Sabbath-breaking, and he pointedly noted that Congregationalists were religious dissenters in the eyes of Anglicans.

Of course Rogers was not always successful in staving off the Congregational rule that overrode English laws. More often than not, he found himself whipped, fined, or imprisoned for breaking Congregational, not English, laws. Rogers seemed to be waging a losing war against the orthodoxy. The biggest impediment to sectarian advances, however, could be attributed to Rogers's own devising. The bottom-line was that increasing religious rights for dissenters was not the main objective for Rogerenes. Rather, Rogers was fixated on spreading his expositions of the Scriptures to New Londoners. He spent a large amount of time with other dissenters, such as the Quakers and Sabbatarians, but he did little to coordinate sectarian advances. Instead, these religious dissenters focused on debating theological matters with one another and how they understood these issues in the light of the Bible.

Issues of salvation and the sacraments dominated Rogerene discussion. In both print and word, Rogers did his best to make his tenets known in New England. Rogers, however, seemed to have generated ideals unsuitable for the New World and only acquired a two-hundred member following at the height of his movement. As the first indigenous sectarian, Rogers had cultivated a radical strain from the Old World Sabbatarians and Quakers, but he had also inherited traditional notions from the Congregationalists. These competing elements did not fare well.

Radicalism for the Rogerenes mostly manifest itself in the rancorous Sabbath demonstrations. During Rogers's tenure as a Sabbatarian, he learned protesting methods and the concept of civil disobedience. When he founded his own sect, he applied these tactics and expanded upon them, so much so that Rogerenes were known for their notorious demonstrations. Such protests were costly since the participants were often fined, whipped, or jailed. A good theological basis was needed to prompt such extremist actions.

Rogerene theology, however, failed to provide an adequate foundation for such rioting. Especially on matters of salvation, which was the most pressing question in colonial times, Rogerenes were very traditional. Much like the Congregationalists, Rogerenes believed in predestination. But subscribing to Calvinist principles posed a significant problem for Rogers. Predestination contradicted the new religious culture that focused on outward obedience as a measure of inward holiness. It alienated many New Englanders who believed that their good works or industry would gain them entrance into heaven. This was coupled with the fact that Congregationalists themselves were less stringent in standards for admitting church members.

Rogers held fast to the importance of internal saintliness despite the changing religious climate. In his desire for a more fervent and Scripture-based faith, Rogers came to believe that a person's conscience should dictate his or her religious course. Matters of conscience gave rise to individualistic actions, such as prizing personal rather than communal prayers and annulling the Sabbath-day observances. New England was a highly communal society, and Rogers's individualistic ordinances created quite a stir. Individualism, however, was never the chief end of Rogerene theology. Instead, it was a byproduct of Rogers's beliefs in reading the Scriptures and following one's conscience. Rogers would never have advocated a society where people lauded individualism for its own sake. For Rogers, pulling away from the larger community and walking a solitary journey were only warranted for the purposeful leading of a holier life faithful to the Scriptures.[18]

John Rogers's life certainly changed the religious milieu in colonial New London. And his writings and actions reverberate into the present day as they inform historians of what religious life looked like in the late seventeenth and early eighteenth centuries. The call to live according to the Scriptures gave meaning to Rogers's life, but he paid dearly to answer that call. He spent years in jail, had large portions of his assets confiscated, and lost his first and most beloved wife. Still, Rogers believed that these losses were Christ's gain and hoped that the world, both Old and New, would one day accept his doctrinal views as truth. His lofty ambitions were sorely frustrated, and the Rogerenes declined

---

[18] The place of Scripture in America before, during, and after Rogers's lifetime can be traced by reading Mark A. Noll, *In the Beginning Was the Word: The Bible in American Public Life, 1492-1783* (New York: Oxford University Press, 2016).

soon after Rogers's death. His doctrines, however, did give rise to ideals that have been instrumental in forming the American consciousness.

Individualism in matters of church and state has become a critical element in the formation of this nation, and faithful obedience to one's conscience has become a valued American religious and civil right. Although the Rogerenes failed to create an enduring denomination, they left a lasting legacy bequeathed in the American culture that lauds individualism and personal conviction. Rogers's reasons for these ideas, however, stemmed from *Sola Scriptura*, rather than any humanitarian or civic impulses that are familiar today. The Bible, and the Bible alone, led Rogers down a unique path that historians are fortunate to uncover.

Notes on Sources

Catherine A. Brekus's sweeping article on the historiography of religion in the United States investigates the "canon" and "countercanon" that undergird the works in this tradition from the nineteenth through the twenty-first centuries.[1] Adopting Martin Marty's usage of this term, the "canon" points to the stories that highlight the powerful influence wielded by the Puritans and the successive generations that have auspiciously combined religion and nationalism.[2] Brekus points to Robert Baird's *Religion in America* as the inaugural work that ushered in more than a century of similar-themed studies focusing on the Protestant mainstream.[3] Such works dominated the field until the 1960s and 1970s when emerged a countercanon built on pluralism of all kinds. The monolithic narrative of Protestant domination was challenged by accounts of gender inequality, racial divides, and denominational proliferation that revealed a fractious and variegated early America.[4]

The canon-countercanon juxtaposition certainly reveals the complexities in both the colonies and their histories. Despite the widening spectrum and inherent nuances, however, this existing historiography fails to comprehensively, and perhaps accurately, delineate the boundaries between orthodoxy and sectarianism. A study of the Rogerenes, for example, greatly challenges this dual canon. The Rogerenes have heretofore been relegated to the countercanon domain for a host of reasons, such as female activism and breaking of the Sabbath. However, a closer

---

[1] Catherine A. Brekus, "Contested Words: History, America, and Religion," *The William and Mary Quarterly* (January 2018, 75, no. 1): 3-36.
[2] Martin Marty (from Breckus) has called this historiographical tradition a "canon" (Martin E. Marty, "The American Religious History Canon," *Social Research* 53, no. 3 (Autumn 1986): 513-28 (quotations, 514).
[3] Robert Baird, *Religion in America* (New York, 1844).
[4] Brekus, "Contested Words," 4-5, 8-9. Brekus also notes Sydney E. Ahlstrom's *A Religious History of the American People* as the "capstone" work that symbolizes Baird's historiographical tradition. One example to substantiate this claim is the "implicit Protestant norm" that is centralized throughout the book and in the description of Catholics and Jews as "countervailing currents." Also, "Western Catholicism" seems to be but a prelude to the "real" religion of Protestantism inaugurated by the Reformation (see Chapters 1-5 in Sydney E. Ahlstrom's *A Religious History of the American People* (New Haven: Yale University Press, 1972), 1-83).

examination of the Rogerenes shows that this sectarian group was one of the staunchest supporters of the validity and inerrancy of Scripture, which certainly resembles the Congregationalists' ethos of *Sola Scriptura*. Rogerene adherence to the Old and New Testaments was not just an accidental or incidental part of their theology. Expounding and living according to the Bible was the very central core tenet that drove this sectarian cause, and their fundamentalism rivaled, if not exceeded, the staunchest of Puritans in their day. Rogerene commitment to the Scriptures provided a quandary for their neighbors and, subsequently, for the historians who have hence examined their words and deeds. This sectarian group proves that sometimes preexisting labels no longer work.

The Rogerenes reveal that the intermix of orthodoxy and sectarianism was messier, more complicated, and more nuanced than historians have thought. Further, the Puritan mind, as well as the soul, defined not just the visible saints but colonists who supposedly reeked of heresy.[5] John Rogers's many writings reflected this Augustinian strain of piety and Ramist logic, and even his ideas about relationships closely follow the patterns explained in the *Dialectica*.[6] Further, the entire Puritan premise that God chose this special people and confirmed their calling through a covenant appears throughout Rogers's writings. One of many examples that expressed similar thinking between Rogers and his orthodox contemporaries is the following excerpt. Using a typical New England form of question-and-answer, Rogers posed his own question: "Why is the Ten Commandments called a Covenant?" He answered his own question with these words: "Because God espoused Israel to himself by that Covenant, so that God was the Head and Husband, and Israel was the Wife, and that Law was the Covenant of her Obedience." Rogers further contended that New Englanders were now this "chosen People," a new Israel in a new Promised Land. Rogers then exhorted his readers to

---

[5] For a full study on the Puritan Mind, see Perry Miller, *The New England Mind: The Seventeenth Century* (Cambridge: Harvard University Press, 1939); and for an explanation of the Puritan soul, see Harry S. Stout, *The New England Soul: Preaching and Religious Culture in Colonial New England* (New York: Oxford University Press, 1986). The term "visible saints" is clearly examined in Edmund S. Morgan, *Visible Saints: The History of a Puritan Idea* (New York: New York University, 1963).

[6] Beyond Miller's own words on Ramus (see *The New England Mind: The Seventeenth Century*, pp. 116-163), Edmund S. Morgan provides a condensed presentation on this complex idea (see Morgan, *The Puritan Family: Religious and Domestic Relations in Seventeenth-Century New England* (New York: Harper & Row, 1944), 21-25).

live piously in New England, a new Canaan, by "deny[ing] Ungodliness & Worldly Lusts, and to live soberly, righteously and godly in this present World."[7] Had Rogers's name not been attributed to this piece, it could have easily passed for the words of Cotton Mather, Gurdon Saltonstall, or any of the Puritan divines of his time.

From upholding the paradigm of a covenant to believing that the Puritans were the new Israel, Rogers fell right in line with the notion that this special group of people were sent on an errand into the wilderness.[8] And Rogers's mission was driven by nothing other than the same Scriptures that the Puritans upheld as the singular source of truth and reason. Rogers stated plainly, "we see this Word was in the beginning with God, and it was God, for in it was life, and it did then proceed from God, and created every creature, as appears by those fore-mentioned verses in [Genesis]."[9] The Scriptures held a central and permanent place in Rogerene theology and also served as the impetus for their entire movement. To attribute modern-day ambitions for Rogerene impulses is to miss their point altogether. Pluralism, individual rights, and increased toleration were anathema to Rogers as much as they were to their orthodox neighbors. Certainly, current notions of liberalism and conservatism were unknown ideals in Rogers's time. The overlap in Rogerene and Congregational thoughts should not be misconstrued or downplayed when assessing the traditional and sectarian premises that have so long defined America's religious past.

All this reveals that the Puritan dilemma has also been the historians' dilemma. The telling of the Puritan story has been as complex as John Winthrop's quandary about the visible saint's obligation to serve God in a world of heretics and heathens.[10] From Perry Miller, Edmund Morgan, and Robert Middlekauff and down through the years, historians have grappled with how to retell the stories of men like John Winthrop and

---

[7] John Rogers, *An Epistle to the Churches of Christ Call'd Quakers* (New York, 1705), 26, 46-47.

[8] Though the Puritans were successful in driving out the likes of Roger Williams, Anne Hutchinson, the Gortonists, and Anabaptists into that "cesspool" known as Rhode Island, Rogers resided in New London until his death. Perry Miller, *Errand Into the Wilderness* (Cambridge: Harvard University Press, 1956), 13.

[9] John Rogers, *A Mid-Night Cry from the Temple of God to the Ten Virgins Slumbering and Sleeping, Awake, Awake, Arise, and Gird Your Loyns, and Trim Your Lamps, for Behold the Bridegroom Cometh, Go Ye Therefore Out to Meet Him* (New London: Green, 1722), 17.

[10] Edmund S. Morgan, *The Puritan Dilemma: The Story of John Winthrop* (Boston: Little Brown, 1958), 5-8.

Richard, Increase, and Cotton Mather, and dissenters like Anne Hutchinson, Roger Williams, and, now, John Rogers.[11] Undoubtedly, the orthodox and antinomian traditions are as long as their telling. Also, the terms *orthodox* and *dissenter* are as messy as the moniker *Puritan*. The two terms are often used in synonymous ways to convey a staunch and static conservatism; but as Sydney Ahlstrom notes, the many "accretions" in the renditions of "Mistress Anne Hutchinson" and her "disturbances in the Bay Colony" paint a very complex picture. In fact, Ahlstrom's usage of the term "amorphous" to describe English sectarianism is altogether appropriate for colonial implications. Just as "archbishops as well as some itinerant Ranters can properly be referred to as Puritans" in England, the theological mirroring between Rogers and the Puritans across the Atlantic shows an uncanny resemblance.[12]

Along with the eminency of Scripture, the jeremiads serve as another parallel between Rogerene thought and that of their Congregationalist contemporaries in both theme and ambition. By the rise of the Rogerenes in the 1660s, the Congregationalists had made compromises, such as the 1662 Half-Way Covenant, that pointed to a troubled, if not failing, errand. In fact, this compromise attested to the fact that since the start, this errand had been fraught with opposition. Decades prior, perhaps soon after John Winthrop disembarked off the *Arabella*, the Puritans faced the reality that even their Promised Land had enemies. The Rogerenes were certainly not the first dissenters to cause a disturbance. Winthrop's life intersected with those he considered profane, and there were seasons when doubt and confusion crept into his mind. Yet, these hardships bade him stay rather than withdraw from society. His dealings with the Anne Hutchinsons of the world only confirmed the necessity for men of his stature to keep God's laws unmolested and keep the course on this divine "errand into the wilderness."[13] Miller's title was taken from Samuel Danforth's election sermon delivered on May 11, 1670, and sermon titles such as this one exposed the seeming "spiritual

---

[11] For an in-depth study of how the Mathers influenced three generations of Puritan life, see Robert Middlekauff, *The Mathers: Three Generations of Puritan Intellectuals, 1596-1728* (Oxford University Press, 1971).

[12] Sydney E. Ahlstrom, "The Problem of the History of Religion in America," *Church History* 39 (1970): 224.

[13] Morgan, *The Puritan Dilemma*, 135.

decay"and "waning resolve" that had settled in by the latter third of the seventeenth century.[14] As Miller notes, Danforth was "fully aware of the ambiguity concealed in his word 'errand'" that revealed deep-seated fears over an errand that had perhaps come to naught.[15]

Ambiguity gave way to ambivalence as noted by historian Bruce C. Daniels. He discusses the "intensely ambivalent culture" within Puritan society, such as the unresolved contentions within the ideals of conformity and liberty.[16] If John Rogers appears ambivalent, this, too, is reminiscent of the world in which he lived. For example, John Rogers also lamented the condition of New England and wrote jeremiads of his own. The theme of declension invaded many of his writings, but perhaps *A Mid-Night Cry from the Temple of God* most aptly conveys this motif that centered around New England's spiritual decline. Rogers bemoaned that those in New England have been "slumbering and sleeping, and thereby neglect[ed] the trim[m]ing of" their faiths are now "but a dull light." Then, Rogers charges his readers to "Awake, Awake, therefore, and arise trim up your lamps, that you may be in a readiness to enter in with the Bridegroom to the Marriage of the Lamb."[17] The succeeding pages combine the curious mix of demise and call-to-arms found in colonial jeremiads.

The timing of the October 19, 1652 fast day ordered by the General Court could be an important contributor to Rogers's thinking. Miller notes that this day may be looked upon as "crucial in American history" since, for the first time, the fast prescription included "provoking sins" such as "worldly mindedness, oppression, & hardhartedness."[18] For about two decades prior to the birth of the Rogerenes, there was an increased focus on internal sins that supposedly caused a curse upon New England society. As Miller notes, this shift from external reasons for fasting, such as wars or natural disasters, now turned to gross intro-

---

[14] Harry S. Stout, *The New England Soul: Preaching and Religious Culture in Colonial New England* (New York: Oxford University Press, 1986), 61-63.

[15] Miller, *Errand into the Wilderness*, 2-6.

[16] Bruce C. Daniels, *Puritans at Play: Leisure and Recreation in Colonial New England* (New York: St. Martin's, 1995), 16.

[17] John Rogers, *A Mid-Night Cry from the Temple of God to the Ten Virgins Slumbering and Sleeping, Awake, Awake, Arise, and Gird Your Loyns, and Trim Your Lamps, for Behold the Bridegroom Cometh, Go Ye Therefore Out to Meet Him* (New London: Green, 1722), 3-4.

[18] Perry Miller, *The New England Mind: From Colony to Province* (Cambridge: Harvard University Press, 1953), 28.

spection. Within "ten years" this specific "formula" was completely fixed in New England minds. Rogers's own writings reflect that the jeremiad mentality had been permanently fixed during the formative years of his theological composition.

Rogers undoubtedly heard his share of fast-day sermons, and there is also a good chance that he read these jeremiads as well.[19] As the historian Francis Caulkins notes, Rogers was the owner of "several chests" filled with books, multiple copies of the Bible, and Bible concordances as well. Not only did he publish his own treatises, Rogers was quick to own any copy of the newest and most popular publications.[20] Perhaps Rogers owned *The Day of Doom*, the famous poetic jeremiad penned by Michael Wigglesworth, which was sold-out after the first 1,800 copies were published in Cambridge in 1662. Noted as the first "runaway best-seller in American literary history," Daniels states that a population of about 65,000 in the New England colonies at this time could not get their hands on this piece fast enough. In fact, this book not only sold out, no extant copies remain from its first publication, and Perry Miller's suspicion is that *The Day of Doom* was literally "read to pieces."[21] Whether it was this or other jeremiads, Rogers most certainly consumed these treatises and wrote his own that reflected this theme of parsing sin and moral failures. The similar motifs in Rogers's and Wigglesworth's works indicate that these minds were cut from the same proverbial cloth.

The jeremiad is but one point of similarity between the Puritans and Rogerenes that indicates that the orthodox-sectarian divide was inextricably interlaced, and the existing historiography leaves room to imagine what the porous religious boundaries in colonial New England could create.[22] An important caveat, however, that historians must heed is to refrain from framing the colonial world to imitate our own. The

---

[19] Books were certainly not inexpensive, yet still approximately half of the seventeenth-century New Englanders had books listed in the probate inventories. Daniels, *Puritans at Play*, 38.

[20] Francis Manwaring Caulkins, *History of New London, Connecticut: From the First Survey of the Coast in 1612, to 1860* (New London: H.D. Utley, 1895), 221.

[21] Bruce Daniels, *Puritans at Play*, 38-39.

[22] For example, see Lockridge's study of colonial Dedham that argues against a monolithic morality. The questions posed by Lockridge of Dedham, such as the "essence of pre-industrial village life" and the concepts of "American[ness]" found in democracy and equalitarianism" can easily be transferred to colonial New London. Kenneth A. Lockridge, *A New England Town: The First Hundred Years* (New York: W.W. Norton & Company, 1970), xiv-xv.

creation of orthodox and sectarian intermingling are not easy precursors to our own world of rights and tolerance. As Beneke and Grenda point out, "the people inhabiting this [colonial] place and time shared our modern understandings of intolerance and tolerance, [and] they did so in the domain of religion."[23] What is surprising, however, is that sectarians such as John Rogers were the staunchest supporters of intolerance and were the last to fight for increased religious toleration. Such unforeseen discoveries, such as these displays of Rogerene orthodoxy, should cause historians to pause and reassess the existing canon. Also, new discoveries can sometimes invite new language in a bid to adequately express a new narrative.

In the current digital age where wordsmithing has hit record highs, new words have appeared more often than in previous generations. Whether in Urban Dictionary or more academically accredited sources, words such as "zoodles (zucchini noodles)," or "glamping (glamorous clamping)" have become a part of the 21st century vernacular as old words, or a combination thereof, define new ideas. In this same vein, a current study of the Rogerenes requires a new usage of old terms: *"sectarian piety."* The word piety has heretofore been largely relegated to orthodox fundamentalists in the colonial age. These people represented the religious elites who tried to tow the line. On the other end of the spectrum were the sectarians who, intentionally or unbeknownst to them, vied for increased toleration and equal treatment before the law. The term *sectarian piety* redraws the lines around these prescribed enclaves and shows why sectarians, such as John Rogers, were deeply pious in their own rights and cared very little about the intrinsic value of increasing rights for dissenters.[24]

In its simplest terms, sectarian piety means that sectarians, like their orthodox counterparts, yearned for religious fervor through traditional means. Scripture and prayer were considered the primary means through which man could understand the mysterious ways of God; and

---

[23] Christ Beneke and Christopher S. Grenda, eds., *The First Prejudice: Religious Tolerance and Intolerance in Early America* (Philadelphia: University of Pennsylvania, 2011), 1.

[24] The idea of increasing rights for dissenters in an effort to create a more tolerant society was not a pursuit of the Rogerenes. This, however, differs from all colonists' passionate desire to protect their rights in general. As Daniels notes, Connecticut towns did their best to remain on good terms with the Mother Country so that their rights and Englishmen would not be curbed. Bruce C. Daniels, T*he Connecticut Town: Growth and Development, 1635-1790* (Middletown: Wesleyan University Press, 1979).

these modes were cherished not just by the Standing Order, but by sectarians such as the Rogerenes. Religious studies of the colonial years in their earliest form often depict sectarians as pursuers of the esoteric, while positioning the orthodoxy as the torchbearers of Scriptural authority and precepts. As Brekus noted, Baird's inaugural work on religion in America set this theme of Protestant uniformity, and sectarians were not invited into the dominant discourse until well into the 20th century.[25]

This discourse has been incredibly robust, and perhaps the fascination with American religion, and the Puritans in particular, can largely be traced back to Perry Miller's seminal work, *The New England Mind: The Seventeenth Century*.[26] After this influential study, historian Charles Lloyd Cohen rightly said, "Of making many books on Puritans there is no end."[27] Since then, the study of those whom the Puritans disdained has also become a vigorous conversation in its own right. And the scholarship from the four decades or so surrounding Miller's influential work also point to both the dualities of orthodoxy and sectarianism.[28] The

---

[25] Besides from Baird's *Religion in America*, some other works to consider in the latter-half of the 19th C are Gideon Hiram Hollister, *The History of Connecticut* (New Haven: Durrie and Peck, 1855); Isaac Backus, *History of New-England with Particular Reference to the Denomination of Christians Called Baptists* (Newton: The Backus Historical Society, 1871); Joseph B. Felt, *The Ecclesiastical History of New England* (Boston, 1862); E. Edwards Beardsley, *The History of the Episcopal Church in Connecticut from the Settlement of the Colony to the Death of Bishop Seabury* (New York: Hurd and Houghton, 1865); Elias B. Sanford, *A History of Connecticut* (Hartford: S.S. Scranton, 1888); Edwin Pond Parker, *History of the Second Church of Christ in Hartford* (Hartford: Belknap and Warfield, 1892); Williston Walker, *The Creeds and Platforms of Congregationalism* (New York: 1893); and David B. Ford, *New England's Struggles for Religious Liberty* (Philadelphia, 1896).

[26] Interesting articles on Miller to consider are Robert Middlekauff, "Perry Miller," in Marcus Cunliffe and Robin W. Winks, eds., *Pastmasters: Some Essays on American Historians* (New York, 1969), 167-90 and David A. Hollinger, "Perry Miller and Philosophical History," *History and Theory* 7 (1968): 189-202.

[27] Charles Lloyd Cohen, *God's Caress: The Psychology of Puritan Religious Experience* (New York: Oxford University Press, 1986), 3.

[28] The following studies, from the 1930s to 1960s, also look at themes of orthodoxy, sectarianism, and the nuances of the Puritan experience: Perry Miller, *Orthodoxy in Massachusetts, 1630-1650* (Cambridge: Harvard University Press, 1933); John M. Mecklin, *The Story of American Dissent* (New York: Harcourt, Brace, 1934); Edmund S. Morgan, "The Puritans and Sex," *New England Quarterly* (Dec. 1942), XV, 591-607; Edmund Morgan, *The Puritan Family: Religion and Domestic Relations in Seventeenth-Century New England* (New York: Harper & Row, 1944); Geoffrey Nuttall, *The Holy Spirit in Puritan Faith and Experience* (Oxford: Blackwell, 1946). Perry Miller, *The New England Mind: From Colony to Province* (Cambridge: Harvard University Press, 1953); Perry Miller, *Roger Williams: His Contribution to the American Tradition* (Indianapolis: Bobbs-Merrill, 1953); Perry Miller, *Errand Into the Wilderness* (Cambridge: Harvard University Press, 1956); Geoffrey Nuttall, *Visible Saints: The Congregational Way, 1640-1660* (Oxford: Blackwell, 1957); Dudley W.R. Bahlman, *The Moral Revolution of 1688* (New Haven: Yale University Press, 1957); Morgan, *The Puritan Dilemma*; George L. Haskins, *Law and Authority in Early Massachusetts* (New York: Macmillan Company, 1960); Carl Bridenbaugh, *Mitre and Sceptre: Transatlantic Faiths, Ideas, Personalities and Politics, 1689-1775* (New York: Oxford University Press, 1962); Edmund S. Morgan, *Visible Saints: The History of a Puritan Idea* (New York: New York University, 1963); Sumner

succeeding decades, primarily in the 1970s and the 1980s, teemed with vigor as fresh angles and new questions were asked of the same Puritans who captured the American imagination earlier in the century. From William G. McLoughlin's study on New England Baptists to the ideas and traditions of radicalism explored independently by Christopher Hill and Philip Gura, historians continued to find new sources to explore old themes.[29] Adding to the scholarship of these years were the important works of Patricia Bonomi and David D. Hall,[30] who both proved that Puritan New England was far more diverse in beliefs and lifestyles than previously recognized.[31]

Chilton Powell, *Puritan Village: The Formation of a New England Town* (Hanover: Wesleyan University Press, 1963); Winthrop S. Hudson, *Religion in America* (New York: Charles Scribner's Sons, 1965); Kai T. Erikson, *Wayward Puritan: A Study in the Sociology of Deviance* (New York: Wiley Press, 1966); Norman Pettit, *The Heart Prepared: Grace and Conversion in Puritan Spiritual Life* (New Haven: Wesleyan University Press, 1966); Marion L. Starkey, *The Congregational Way: The Role of the Pilgrims and Their Heirs in Shaping America* (Garden City: Doubleday, 1966); William G. McLoughlin, *Isaac Backus and the American Pietistic Tradition* (Boston: Little, Brown, 1967); Edmund S. Morgan, *Roger Williams: The Church and the State* (New York: W.W. Norton & Company, 1967); Barton J. Bernstein, ed. *Towards a New Past: Dissenting Essays in American History* (New York: Random House, 1968); Mary Jeanne Anderson Jones, *Congregational Commonwealth: Connecticut, 1636-1662* (Middletown: Wesleyan University Press, 1968); Paul A. Carter, "Recent Historiography of the Protestant Churches in America," *Church History* 37 (1968): 95-107; Robert G. Pope, *The Half-Way Covenant: Church Membership in Puritan New England* (Princeton: Princeton University Press, 1969).

[29] William G. McLoughlin, *New England Dissent: The Baptists and the Separation of Church and State, 1630-1833* (Cambridge: Harvard University Press, 1971); Christopher Hill, *The World Turned Upside Down: Radical Ideas During the English Revolution* (New York: Penguin Books, 1972); Philip F. Gura, *A Glimpse of Sion's Glory: Puritan Radicalism in New England, 1620-1660* (Middletown: Wesleyan University Press, 1984); David S. Lovejoy, *Religious Enthusiasm in the New World: Heresy to Revolution* (Cambridge: Harvard University Press, 1985).

[30] Patricia Bonomi, *Under the Cope of Heaven: Religion, Society, and Politics in Colonial America* (New York: Oxford University Press, 1986) and David D. Hall, *Worlds of Wonder, Days of Judgement: Popular Religious Belief in Early New England* (Cambridge: Harvard University Press, 1989).

[31] Additional works to consider from the 1970s and 1980s are: Philip J. Greven, *Four Generations: Population, Land, and Family in Colonial Andover, Massachusetts* (Ithaca, N.Y.: Cornell University Press, 1970); John Demos, *A Little Commonwealth: Family Life in Plymouth Colony* (New York: Oxford University Press, 1970);, Kenneth A. Lockridge, *A New England Town, the First Hundred Years: Dedham, Massachusetts, 1636-1736* (New York, 1970); George M. Marsden "Perry Miller's Rehabilitation of the Puritans: A Critique," *Church History*, 39 (1970): 91-105; Michael. Zuckerman, *Peaceable Kingdoms: New England Towns in the Eighteenth Century* (New York, 1970); Robert Middlekauff, *The Mathers: Three Generations of Puritan Intellectuals, 1596-1728* (Oxford University Press, 1971); Sydney A. Ahlstrom, *Religious History of the American People* (New Haven: Yale University Press, 1972; David D. Hall, *The Faithful Shepherd: A History of the New England Ministry in the Seventeenth Century* (Chapel Hill, N.C., 1972), 115–120; William T. Youngs, Jr., "Congregational Clericalism: New England Ordinations Before the Great Awakening," *William and Mary Quarterly*, XXXI (1974), 481–490; George M. Marsden and Frank Roberts, eds., *A Christian View of History?* (Grand Rapids: Eerdmans, 1975); Daniel Scott Smith and Michael S. Hindus, "Premarital Pregnancy in America, 1640–1971: An Overview and Interpretation," *Journal of Interdisciplinary History*, V (1975), 537–570; Baird Tipson, "Invisible Saints: The 'Judgment of Charity' in the Early New England Churches," *Church History*, XLIV (1975), 460; Paul R. Lucas, *Valley of Discord: Church and Society along the Connecticut River, 1636-1725* (Hanover, H.H.: University Press of New England, 1976);

The decades that flanked the 21st century also produced scholarship pushing the boundaries of orthodoxy and sectarianism. From the occult to the plurality of American religious origins, Butler's study opened new dialogue about American Christianity.[32] And Carla Pestana's work on religion, highlighting both dissenting and fundamentalist traditions, added greatly to the existing dialogue.[33] The works produced alongside these writings are especially helpful in better understanding where the Rogerenes fit into this discourse.[34] Currently, this niche group

---

Francis J. Bremer, *The Puritan Experiment: New England Society from Bradford to Edwards* (New York: St. Martin's, 1976); Laurel Thatcher Ulrich, "Virtuous Women Found: New England Ministerial Literature, 1668–1735," *American Quarterly*, XXVIII (1976), 22–23; David E. Stannard, *The Puritan Way of Death: A Study in Religion, Culture, and Social Change* (New York: Oxford University Press, 1977); Philip D. Zimmerman, "The Lord's Supper in Early New England: The Setting and the Service," in Peter Benes, ed., *New England Meeting House and Church: 1630–1850, Dublin Seminar for New England Folklife, Annual Proceedings* 1979 (Boston, 1979), 130–133; Rodney Stark and William Sims Bainbridge. "Networks of Faith: Interpersonal Bonds and Recruitment to Cults and Sects," *American Journal of Sociology* 85 (1980): 1376-95; Charles E. Hambrick-Stowe, *The Practice of Piety: Puritan Devotional Disciplines in Seventeenth-Century New England* (Chapel Hill, N.C., 1982), 208–217; John Waters, "Family, Inheritance, and Migration in Colonial New England: The Evidence from Guilford, Connecticut," *William and Mary Quarterly*, XXXIX (1982), 64–86; Patricia Caldwell, *The Puritan Conversion Narrative: The Beginnings of American Expression* (Cambridge, 1983), 45–116; Philip F. Gura, *A Glimpse of Sion's Glory: Puritan Radicalism in New England, 1620-1660* (Middletown: Wesleyan University Press, 1984); Jackson Turner Main, *Society and Economy in Colonial Connecticut* (Princeton, N.J., 1985); Sidney Mead, *The Nation with the Soul of A Church* (Macon, Ga., 1985); Jan Shipps, *Mormonism: The Story of a New Religious Tradition* (Urbana: University of Illinois Press, 1985); Martin E. Marty, "The American Religious History Canon," *Social Research* 53, no. 3 (Autumn 1986): 513-28; John Demos, *Past, Present, and Personal: The Family and the Life Course in American History* (New York, 1986), 139–185; R. Laurence Moore, *Religious Outsiders and the Making of Americans* (New York: Oxford University Press, 1986); David D. Hall, "On Common Ground: The Coherence of American Puritan Studies," *William and Mary Quarterly*, XLIV (1987), 213–222; Nicholas Canny and Anthony Pagden, eds., *Colonial Identity in the Atlantic World, 1500-1800* (Princeton: Princeton University Press, 1987); Wuthnow, Robert. *The Restructuring of American Religion* (Princeton: Princeton University Press, 1988); Henry Warner Bowden, "The Historiography of American Religion, in Charles Lippy and Peter Williams, eds., *Encyclopedia of the American Religious Experience* 3 vols. (New York, 1989); Nathan O. Hatch, *The Democratization of American Christianity* (New Haven: Yale University Press, 1989); Harry S. Stout, "Theological Commitment and American Religious History," *Theological Education*, 25 (1989), 44-59; Baird Tipson, "Samuel Stone's 'Discourse' against Requiring Church Relations," *William and Mary Quarterly*, XLVI (1989), 786–799.

[32] Jon Butler, *Awash in a Sea of Faith: Christianizing the American Past* (Cambridge: Harvard University Press, 1990).

[33] Amongst her many works, these two in particular helped shape my study on the Rogerenes: Carla G. Pestana, *Quakers and Baptists in Colonial Massachusetts* (New York: Cambridge University Press, 1991) and Carla G. Pestana, "Religion," in David Armitage and Michael J. Braddick, eds., *The British Atlantic World, 1500-1800* (New York: Palgrave Macmillan, 2002): 69-89.

[34] Additional works to consider are: John Corrigan, *The Prism of Piety: Catholick Congregational Clergy at the Beginning of the Enlightenment, Religion in America* (New York: Oxford University Press, 1991); Stephen Foster, *The Long Argument: English Puritanism and the Shaping of New England Culture, 1570–1700* (Chapel Hill: University of North Carolina Press, 1991); Laurel Thatcher Ulrich, *Good Wives: Image and Reality in the Lives of Women in Northern New England, 1650-1750* (New York: Vintage, 1991); Gerald F.

has been relegated as just that, marginal and insignificant to the New England landscape. These robust studies, however, show that the ideas of marginalization have equally been debated as the marginalized themselves. Rogers's own words add to this concept of marginalization, es-

---

Moran and Maris A. Vinovskis, "The Puritan Family and Religion: A Critical Reappraisal," in Moran and Vinovskis, eds., *Religion, Family, and the Life Course: Explorations in the Social History of Early America* (Ann Arbor: University of Michigan Press, 1992), 26–27; Richard Godbeer, T*he Devil's Dominion: Magic and Religion in Early New England* (Cambridge: Cambridge University Press, 1992); Francis J. Bremer, ed., *Puritanism: Transatlantic Perspectives on a Seventeenth-Century Anglo-American Faith* (Boston: Massachusetts Historical Society, 1993; John Demos, *The Unredeemed Captive: A Family Story from Early America* (New York: Vintage Books, 1994); Janice Knight, *Orthodoxies in Massachusetts: Rereading American Puritanism* (Cambridge: Harvard University Press, 1994); Richard P. Gildrie, *The Profane, the Civil, and the Godly: The Reformation of Manners in Orthodox New England, 1679–1749* (University Park: Penn State University Press, 1994); Mark A. Noll, George M. Rawlyk, and David W. Bebbington, eds., *Evangelicalism: Comparative Studies of Popular Protestantism of North America and the British Isles, 1700-1990* (New York: Oxford University Press, 1994); Daniels, *Puritans at Play* (1995); Richard Godbeer, "'Love Raptures': Marital, Romantic, and Erotic Images of Jesus Christ in Puritan New England, 1670–1730," *New England Quarterly*, LXVIII (1995), 355–384; Daniel Scott Smith and J. David Hacker, "Cultural Demography: New England Deaths and the Puritan Perception of Risk," *Journal of Interdisciplinary History,* XXVI (1996), 380–383; Rodney Stark and William Sims Bainbridge. *A Theory of Religion* (New Brunswick: Rutgers University Press, 1996); Michael P. Winship, *Seers of God: Puritan Providentialism in the Restoration and Early Enlightenment, Early America: History, Context, Culture* (Baltimore: Johns Hopkins University, 1996); David D. Hall, "Narrating Puritanism," in Harry S. Stout and D. G. Hart, eds., *New Directions in American Religious History* (New York, 1997), 67–68; Mark A. Peterson, *The Price of Redemption: The Spiritual Economy of Puritan New England* (Palo Alto: Stanford University Press, 1997); David D. Hall, ed., *Lived Religion in America: Toward a History of Practice* (Princeton: Princeton University Press, 1997); Harry S. Stout and Robert M. Taylor, Jr. "Studies of Religion in American Society: The State of the Art," *New Directions in American Religious History*, edited by Harry S. Stout and D.G. Hart (New York: Oxford University Press, 1997); Erik R. Seeman, "Lay Conversion Narratives: Investigating Ministerial Intervention," *New England Quarterly*, LXXI (1998), 629–634; Lisa Wilson, *Ye Heart of a Man: The Domestic Life of Men in Colonial New England* (New Haven: Yale University Press, 1999); Rodney Stark and Roger Finke. *Acts of Faith: Explaining the Human Side of Religion* (Berkeley: University of California Press, 2000); Gloria L. Main, *Peoples of a Spacious Land: Families and Cultures in Colonial New England* (Cambridge: Harvard University Press, 2001); Mark A. Peterson, "Puritanism and Refinement in Early New England: Reflections on Communion Silver," *William and Mary Quarterly*, LVIII (2001), 307–346; Mark A. Noll, *America's God: From Jonathan Edwards to Abraham Lincoln* (New York: Oxford University Press, 2002); Michael P. Winship, *Making Heretics: Militant Protestantism and Free Grace in Massachusetts, 1636–1641* (Princeton: Princeton University Press, 2002); E. Brooks. Holifield, *Theology in America: Christian Thought from the Age of the Puritans to the Civil War* (New Haven: Yale University Press, 2003); Carla Gardina Pestana, *The English Atlantic in an Age of Revolution, 1640-1661* (Cambridge: Harvard University Press, 2004); Winnifred Fallers Sullivan, *The Impossibility of Religious Freedom* (Princeton: Princeton University Press, 2005); Laurie F. Maffly-Kipp, Leigh E. Schmidt, and Mark Valeri, eds. *Practicing Protestants: Histories of Christian Life in America, 1630-1965* (Baltimore: Johns Hopkins University Press, 2006); Douglas L. Winiarski, "Religious Experiences in New England," in Amanda Porterfield, ed., *Modern Christianity to 1900, A People's History of Christianity*, VI (Minneapolis: Fortress Press, 2007), 209–232; Douglas L. Winiarski, "Gendered 'Relations' in Haverhill, Massachusetts, 1719–1742," in Peter Benes, ed., *In Our Own Words: New England Diaries, 1600 to the Present, I, Diary Diversity, Coming of Age, Annual Proceedings 2006–2007* (Boston: Dublin Seminar for New England Folklife, 2009), 66–67; Andrew R. Murphy, *Prodigal Nation: Moral Decline and Divine Punishment from New England to 9/11* (New York: Oxford University Press, 2009).

pecially given that the thoughts he penned are surprisingly similar to the most orthodox of New England minds. And his words should be added to this current discourse on what constitutes credibility in defining the American religious experience.[35] ∎

---

[35] Chris Beneke and Christopher S. Grenda, eds. *The First Prejudice: Religious Tolerance and Intolerance in Early America* (Philadelphia: University of Pennsylvania Press, 2011); Catherine A. Brekus and W. Clark Gilpin, eds. *American Christianities: A History of Dominance and Diversity* (Chapel Hill: University of North Carolina Press, 2011); Laura M. Chmielewski, *The Spice of Popery: Converging Christianities on an Early American Frontier* (Notre Dame: University of Notre Dame Press, 2012); David F. Holland, *Sacred Borders: Continuing Revelation and Canonical Restraint in Early America* (New York, Oxford University Press, 2011); Sarah Rivett, *The Science of the Soul in Colonial New England* (Chapel Hill: University of North Carolina Press, 2011); Michael P. Winship, "Congregational Hegemony in New England, from the 1680s to the 1730s," in Stephen J. Stein, ed., *The Cambridge History of Religions in America, I, Pre-Columbian Times to 1790* (Cambridge: Cambridge University Press, 2012), 282–302; Stephanie Kirk and Sarah Rivett, eds. *Religious Transformations in the Early Modern Americas* (Philadelphia: University of Pennsylvania Press, 2014); Sally M. Promey, *Sensational Religion: Sensory Cultures in Material Practice* (New Haven: Yale University Press, 2014); Randall J. Pederson, *Unity in Diversity: English Puritans and the Puritan Reformation, 1603-1689* (Leiden: Brill, 2014); Amy Hollywood, *Acute Melancholia and Other Essays: Mysticism, History, and the Study of Religion* (New York: Columbia University Press, 2016); Susan Juster, *Sacred Violence in Early America* (Philadelphia: University of Pennsylvania Press, 2016); Robert A. Orsi, *History and Presence* (Cambridge: Harvard University Press, 2016); Douglas L. Winiarski, *Darkness Falls on the Land of Light: Experiencing Religious Awakenings in Eighteenth-Century New England* (Chapel Hill: University of North Carolina Press, 2017).

Bibliography

Manuscript Sources

Connecticut State Archives, Connecticut State Library, Hartford, Connecticut.
>Connecticut Archives. Microfilm.
>>Court Papers, 1649-1709, Volume 9.
>>Crimes and Misdemeanors, Volumes I & II.
>>Ecclesiastical Affairs, 1st Series (1662-1789).
>>First Congregational Church, New London, Connecticut. 1670-1916.
>>Foreign Correspondence, 1st Series (1661-1748), 2nd Series (1666-1768).
>>Private Controversies, 1st Series, 2nd Series (1636-1811).

>Court Records
>>Superior Court Records, 1718-1725.
>>New London County Court Files, 1691-1722.
>>New London County Court Records of Trials. 1689-1703.
>>New London County Court Superior Court Files, 1711-1724.
>>New London Grand Jury Records, 1700-1701.

Primary Sources

Bolles, John. *An Answer of Confutation upon the Articles of the Confession of Faith*. New London: n.p., 1731.

Bownas, Samuel. *The Life, Travels, and Christian Experiences of Samuel Bownas*. Linfield: The Schools of Industry, 1836.

Clark, Samuel. *A Brief concordance to the Holy Bible, of the most usual and useful places which one may have occasion to see for in a new method*. London: T. Parkhurst, 1696.

Edmundson, William. *A Journal of the Life, Travels, Sufferings, and Labour of Love in the Work of the Ministry, of that Worthy Elder and Faithful Servant of Jesus Christ, William Edmundson, Who Departed this Life, the Thirty-first of the Sixth Month, 1712*, 3rd ed. Dublin: Christopher Bentham, 1820.

Fitch, James. *An Explanation of the Solemn Advice, Recommended by the Council in Connecticut Colony*. Boston: Green, 1683.

Hempstead, Joshua. *Diary of Joshua Hempstead of New London, Connecticut: Covering a Period of Forty-Seven Years from September 1711 to November 1758*. New London: The New London Historical Society, 1901.

Peter Pratt, Jr., T*he Prey Taken from the Strong. Or, An historical acount, of the recovery of one from the dangerous errors of Quakerism. An account of the principal articles of the Quaker faith, and especially of the New London Quakers the disciples of John Rogers. As also, a brief answer to John Rogers's boasting of his sufferings for his conscience, &c. With a word of advice to all who adhere to those doctrines* (New London: T. Green, 1725).

Powell, Vavasor. *A New and Useful Concordance to the Holy Bible. Where unto is added, the chief acceptations & various significations contained in the Old and New Testament. Also a collection of those Scripture-prophesies which relate to the call of the Jews*. London: R. Clark, 1671.

John Rogers, *An Answer to a Book Intituled, The Lords Day Proved to be the Christian Sabbath &c. By B. Wadsworth, A.M. Pastor of a Church in Boston. And also, An Answer to a Pamphlet, Intituled Thesis concerning the Sabbath. As Also, Some Part of what hath passed through the General Courts in Connecticut Colony, relating to the Sabbath. As Also, Some Court Sentences* in that Colony, by John Rogers. Boston: n.p., 1721.

___. *An Epistle to the Churches of Christ call'd Quakers; And another epistle to the Seventh Day Baptists, with several Theological Es says.* New York: William Bradford, 1705.

___. *John Rogers a Servant of Jesus Christ, to any of the Flock of Christ that may be scattered among the Churches of New-England, Greeting,* 4th ed. Norwich: n.p., 1776.

___. *An Epistle Sent from God to the World, containing the Best News that ever the World Heard. And transcribed by John Rogers, a Servant of Jesus Christ.* New York: Printed for Elisha Stanbury, 1720/1.

___. *An Impartial Relation of an Open and Publick Dispute Agreed upon Between Gurdon Saltonstall, Minister of the Town of New-London, and John Rogers of the Same Place.* Philadelphia: Reynier Jansen, 1701.

___. *A Mid-Night Cry from the Temple of God to the Ten Virgins Slum bering and Sleeping, Awake, Awake, Arise, and gird your Loyns, and trim your Lamps, for behold the Bridegroom cometh, go ye therefore out to meet him.* New London: Green, 1722.

___. *The Book of the Revelation of Jesus Christ, which God gave unto him: to show unto his servants things which were to come to pass; and Jesus Christ sent and signified it by his angels to his servant John; and now by revelation, hath opened the mystery contained in said book, unto his servant John Rogers, of his Church and People, after a long and dark night of apostacy. The explanation being made so plain, that they eye of every spiritual reader may see how exactly things have come to pass, as were foretold by the Prophecy of this Book: and may see by it all things which are yet to come, not only to the end of this*

World but to the finishing of the World to come. Boston: n.p., 1720.

Rogers, Jr., John. *An Answer to a Book Lately Put Forth by Peter Pratt, Entituled, The Prey Taken from the Strong. Wherein by Mocks and Scoffs, together with a great number of positive Falshoods, the Author hath greatly abused John Rogers, late of New-London, deceased, since his Death.* New York: n.p., 1726.

Saltonstall, Gurdon. *A Sermon Preached before the General Assembly of the Colony of Connecticut at Hartford in New England, May 13, 1697, being the Day for Electing the Governour, Depty Governour and Assistants, for that Colony*. Boston: B. Green and J. Allen, 1697.

Shepard, Thomas. *The Works of Thomas Shepard*. Boston: Doctrinal Tract and Book Society, 1853.

Wadsworth, Benjamin. *The Lord's Day, Proved to be the Christian Sabbath. Or Reasons Showing Why the First Day of the Week (called the Lord's Day) should be kept holy as the Christian Sabbath*. Boston: B. Green, 1720.

Secondary Sources

Ahlstrom, Sydney A. "The Problem of the History of Religion in Amerca," *Church History* 39 (1970): 224-35.

____. *Religious History of the American People*. New Haven: Yale University Press, 1972.

Andrews, Charles McLean. *The Colonial Period of American History*, vol. 2. New Haven: Yale University Press, 1936.

____. *Connecticut's Place in Colonial History* (New Haven: Yale University Press for the Connecticut Society of Colonial Wars, (1923).

Atwater, Edward E. *History of the Colony of New Haven to Its Absorption Into Connecticut.* Meriden: Journal Publishing, 1902.

Backus, Isaac. *A History of New-England With Particular Reference to the Denomination of Christians Called Baptists.* Newton: The Backus Historical Society, 1871.

Bahlman, Dudley W.R. *The Moral Revolution of 1688.* New Haven: Yale University Press, 1957.

Bailyn, Bernard. *The New England Merchants In The Seventeenth Century.* New York: Harper & Row, 1955.

Baird, Robert. *Religion in America.* New York: Harper and Brothers, 1844.

Beardsley, E. Edwards. *The History of the Episcopal Church in Connecticut from the Settlement of the Colony to the Death of Bishop Seabury.* New York: Hurd and Houghton, 1865.

Beneke, Chris and Christopher S. Grenda, eds. *The First Prejudice: Religious Tolerance and Intolerance in Early America.* Philadelphia: University of Pennsylvania, 2011.

Bernstein, Barton J., ed. *Towards a New Past: Dissenting Essays in American History.* New York: Random House, 1968.

Blake, Leroy S. *The Early History of the First Church of Christ in New London, Connecticut.* New London: Press of the Day Publishing Company, 1897.

Bolles, John R. and Anna B. Williams. *The Rogerenes: Some Hitherto Unpublished Annals Belonging to the Colonial History of Connecticut.* Boston: Stanhope Press, 1904.

Bonomi, Patricia U. *Under the Cope of Heaven: Religion, Society, and*

Politics in Colonial America. New York: Oxford University Press, 1986.

Bowden, Henry Warner. "The Historiography of American Religion, in Charles Lippy and Peter Williams, eds., *Encyclopedia of the American Religious Experience* 3 vols. New York, 1989.

Brekus, Catherine A. "Contested Words: History, America, and Religion" in T*he William and Mary Quarterly* (January 2018, 75, no 1): 3-36.

Brekus, Catherine A. and W. Clark Gilpin, eds. *American Christianities: A History of Dominance and Diversity*. Chapel Hill: University of North Carolina Press, 2011.

Bremer, Francis J. *The Puritan Experiment: New England Society from Bradford to Edwards*. New York: St. Martin's, 1976.

Bremer, Francis J., ed., *Puritanism: Transatlantic Perspectives on a Seventeenth-Century Anglo-American Faith*. Boston: Massachusetts Historical Society, 1993.

Bridenbaugh, Carl. *Mitre and Sceptre: Transatlantic Faiths, Ideas, Personalities and Politics, 1689-1775*. New York: Oxford University Press, 1962.

Brinton, Ellen Starr. *Books By and About the Rogerenes*. New York: Reprinted from The New York Public Library *Bulletin*, 1945.

___. "The Rogerenes." *New England Quarterly* 16, no. 1 (1943): 2-19.

Brooke, John L. *The Refiner's Fire: The Make of Mormon Cosmology, 1644-1844*. Cambridge: Cambridge University Press, 1994.

Bushman, Richard L. *From Puritan to Yankee: Character and the Social Order in Connecticut, 1690-1765*. Cambridge:

Harvard University Press, 1967.

Caldwell, Patricia. *The Puritan Conversion Narrative: The Beginnings of American Expression*. Cambridge: Cambridge University Press, 1983.

Canny, Nicholas and Anthony Pagden, eds., *Colonial Identity in the Atlantic World, 1500-1800*. Princeton: Princeton University Press, 1987.

Carter, Paul A. "Recent Historiography of the Protestant Churches in America," *Church History* 37 (1968): 95-107.

Caulkins, Frances Manwaring. H*istory of New London, Connecticut: From the First Survey of the Coast in 1612, to 1860*. New London: H.D. Utley, 1895.

Chmielewski, Laura M. The Spice of Popery: Converging Christianities on an Early American Frontier. Notre Dame: University of Notre Dame Press, 2012.

Chu, Jonathan M. *Neighbors, Friends, or Madmen: The Puritan Adjustment to Quakerism in Seventeenth-Century Massachusetts Bay*. Westport: Greenwood Press, 1985.

Clark, George L. *A History of Connecticut: Its People and Institutions*. New York: G.P Putnam's Sons, 1914.

Cohen, Charles Lloyd. *God's Caress: The Psychology of Puritan Religious Experience*. New York: Oxford University Press, 1986.

Cohn, Henry S. "Connecticut's Divorce Mechanism: 1636-1969." *American Journal of Legal History*, XLIV (1970): 35-54.

Corrigan, John. *The Prism of Piety: Catholick Congregational Clergy at the Beginning of the Enlightenment, Religion in America*.

New York: Oxford University Press, 1991.

Cowing, Cedric B. *The Saving Remnant, Religion and the Settling of New England*. Urbana: University of Illinois Press, 1995.

Crane, Elaine Forman. *Ebb Tide in New England: Women, Seaports, and Social Change, 1630-1800*. Boston: Northeastern University Press, 1998.

Daniels, Bruce C. T*he Connecticut Town: Growth and Development, 1635-1790.* Middletown: Wesleyan University Press, 1979.

___. *Puritans at Play: Leisure and Recreation in Colonial New England.* New York: St. Martin's, 1995.

Demos, John. *The Unredeemed Captive: A Family Story from Early America* (New York: Vintage Books, 1994).

Dayton, Cornelia Hughes. *Women before the Bar: Gender, Law, & Society in Connecticut, 1639-1789*. Chapel Hill: The University of North Carolina Press, 1995.

Demos, John. *A Little Commonwealth: Family Life in Plymouth Colony.* New York: Oxford University Press, 1970.

___. *Past, Present, and Personal: The Family and the Life Course in American History*. New York: Oxford University Press, 1986.

Degnan, Francis J. *A New Look at Old New Haven*. New Haven: Yale-New Haven Teachers Institute, 1992.

Dunn, Richard S. *Puritans and Yankees: The Winthrop Dynasty of New England, 1630-1717*. New York: The Norton Library, 1971.

Erikson, Kai T. *Wayward Puritan: A Study in the Sociology of Deviance.* New York: Wiley Press, 1966.

Felt, Joseph B. *The Ecclesiastical History of New England*. Boston: Congregational Library Association, 1862.

Ford, David B. *New England's Struggles for Religious Liberty*. Philadelphia:American Baptist Publication Society, 1896.

Foster, Stephen. T*he Long Argument: English Puritanism and the Shaping of New England Culture, 1570–1700*. Chapel Hill: University of North Carolina Press, 1991.

Frech, Mary L. and William F. Swindler, eds. *Chronology and Documentary Handbook of the State of Connecticut*. Dobbs Ferry: Oceana Publications, Inc., 1973.

Gates, Gilman C. *Saybrook at the Mouth of Connecticut: The First One Hundred Years*. Orange: Wilson H. Lee, 1935.

Gildrie, Richard P. *The Profane, the Civil, and the Godly: The Reformation of Manners in Orthodox New England, 1679–1749*. University Park: Penn State University Press, 1994.

Godbeer, Richard. *The Devil's Dominion: Magic and Religion in Early New England*. Cambridge: Cambridge University Press, 1992.

___. "'Love Raptures': Marital, Romantic, and Erotic Images of Jesus Christ in Puritan New England, 1670–1730," *New England Quarterly*, LXVIII (1995), 355–384.

Greene, Maria Louise. T*he Development of Religious Liberty in Connecticut*. Boston: Houghton, Mifflin, and Company, 1905.

Greven, Philip J. *Four Generations: Population, Land, and Family in Colonial Andover, Massachusetts*. Ithaca: Cornell University Press, 1970.

Grosskopf, Jan Schenk. "Family, Religion, and Disorder: The Rogerenes of New London, 1676-1726." *Connecticut History* 40 (2001): 203 - 224.

Gura, Philip F. *A Glimpse of Sion's Glory: Puritan Radicalism in New England, 1620-1660*. Middletown: Wesleyan University Press, 1984.

Hall, David D. *The Faithful Shepherd: A History of the New England Ministry in the Seventeenth Century*. Chapel Hill: University of North Carolina Press, 1972.

---. "Narrating Puritanism," in Harry S. Stout and D. G. Hart, eds., *New Directions in American Religious History* (New York: Oxford University Press, 1997), 67–68.

___."On Common Ground: The Coherence of American Puritan Studies," *William and Mary Quarterly*, XLIV (1987), 213–222.

___. *Worlds of Wonder, Days of Judgment: Popular Religious Belief in Early New England*. Cambridge: Harvard University Press, 1989.

Hall, David D. ed. *Lived Religion in America: Toward a History of Practice*. Princeton: Princeton University Press, 1997.

Hambrick-Stowe, Charles E. T*he Practice of Piety: Puritan Devotional Disciplines in Seventeenth-Century New England*. Chapel Hill: University of North Carolina Press, 1982.

Haskins, George L. Haskins. *Law and Authority in Early Massachusetts*. New York: Macmillan Company, 1960.

Hatch, Nathan O. *The Democratization of American Christianity.* New Haven: Yale University Press, 1989.

Holifield, E. Brooks. *The Covenant Sealed: The Development of Puritan Sacramental Theology in Old and New England, 1570–1720*. New Haven: Yale University Press, 1974.

___. T*heology in America: Christian Thought from the Age of the Puritans to the Civil War*. New Haven: Yale University Press, 2003.

Holland, David F. *Sacred Borders: Continuing Revelation and Canonical Restraint in Early America*. New York, Oxford University Press, 2011.

Hollinger, David A. "Perry Miller and Philosophical History," *History and Theory* 7 (1968): 189-202.

Hollister, Gideon Hiram. *The History of Connecticut*. New Haven: Durrie and Peck, 1855.

Hollywood, Amy. *Acute Melancholia and Other Essays: Mysticism, History, and the Study of Religion*. New York: Columbia University Press, 2016.

Hudson, Winthrop S. *Religion in America*. New York: Charles Scribner's Sons, 1965.

Jones, Mary Jeanne Anderson. *Congregational Commonwealth: Connecticut, 1636-1662*. Middletown: Wesleyan University Press, 1968.

Juster, Susan. *Sacred Violence in Early America*. Philadelphia: Univesity of Pennsylvania Press, 2016.

Kerber, Linda K. *Women of the Republic: Intellect and Ideology in Revolutionary America*. Chapel Hill: University of North Carolina Press, 1980.

Kirk, Stephanie and Sarah Rivett, eds. *Religious Transformations in the Early Modern Americas*. Philadelphia: University of Pennsylvania Press, 2014.

Knapp, Lewis G. *In Pursuit of Paradise: History of the Town of Stratford, Connecticut.* West Kennewbunk: Phoenix, 1923.

Knight, Janice. *Orthodoxies in Massachusetts: Rereading American Puritanism.* Cambridge: Harvard University Press, 1994.

Ladwig, Julie Q. "Few Traces Remain of Ledyard's Early Dissenters." *Compass Comment* 2, 20.38 (Sept. 18, 1975): 4.

Lee, W. Storrs. *The Yankees of Connecticut.* New York: Henry Hold and Company, 1957.

Lim, Susan. "Evangelization in Print: The Writings of the Rogerenes of New London, 1677-1721." *Connecticut History* 51, no. 2 (2012): 234-250.

___. "The Rise of the Rogerenes in Colonial New London." *Connecticut History* 47, no. 2 (2008): 237-48.

Lockridge, Kenneth A. *A New England Town, the First Hundred Years: Dedham, Massachusetts, 1636-1736.* New York: W.W. Norton & Company, 1970.

Lucas, Paul R. V*alley of Discord: Church and Society along the Connecticut River, 1636-1725.* Hanover: University Press of New England, 1976.

Maffly-Kipp, Laurie F., Leigh E. Schmidt, and Mark Valeri, eds. *Practicing Protestants: Histories of Christian Life in America, 1630-1965.* Baltimore: Johns Hopkins University Press, 2006.

Main, Gloria L. *Peoples of a Spacious Land: Families and Cultures in Colonial New England.* Cambridge: Harvard University

Press, 2001.

Main, Jackson Turner. *Society and Economy in Colonial Connecticut.* Princeton: Princeton University Press, 1985.

Marsden, George M. "Perry Miller's Rehabilitation of the Puritans: A Critique," *Church History,* 39 (1970): 91-105.

Marsden, George M. and Frank Roberts, eds., *A Christian View of History?* Grand Rapids: Eerdmans, 1975.

Marty, Martin E. "The American Religious History Canon," *Social Research* 53, no. 3 (Autumn 1986): 513-28.

Mason, Louis B. *The Life and Times of Major John Mason of Connecticut, 1600-1672.* New York: G.P. Putnam's Sons, 1935.

Mead, Sidney E. *The Lively Experiment: The Shaping of Christianity in America.* New York: Harper & Row, 1963.

___. The Nation with the Soul of A Church. Macon: Mercer University Press, 1985.

McLoughlin, William G. *New England Dissent, 1630-1833: The Baptists and the Separation of Church and State.* Cambridge: Harvard University Press, 1971.

___. *Isaac Backus and the American Pietistic Tradition.* Boston: Little Brown, 1967.

Mecklin, John M. *The Story of American Dissent.* New York: Harcourt, Brace, 1934.

Middlekauff, Robert. T*he Mathers: Three Generations of Puritan Intellectuals, 1596-1728.* Oxford University Press, 1971.

____. "Perry Miller." In *Pastmasters: Some Essays on American Historians*, edited by Marcus Cunliffe and Robin W. Winks, 167-190. New York: Harper, 1969.

Miller, Perry. *Errand Into the Wilderness*. Cambridge: Harvard University Press, 1956.

____. *The New England Mind: From Colony to Province*. Cambridge: Harvard University Press, 1953.

____. *The New England Mind: The Seventeenth Century*. Cambridge: Harvard University Press, 1939.

____. *Orthodoxy in Massachusetts, 1630-1650*. Cambridge: Harvard University Press, 1933.

____. R*oger William: His Contribution to the American Tradition*. Indianapolis: Bobbs-Merrill, 1953.

Moore, R. Laurence. *Religious Outsiders and the Making of Americans*. New York: Oxford University Press, 1986.

Moran, Gerald F. and Maris A. Vinovskis, "The Puritan Family and Religion: A Critical Reappraisal," in Moran and Vinovskis, eds., *Religion, Family, and the Life Course: Explorations in the Social History of Early America* (Ann Arbor: University of Michigan Press, 1992), 26–27.

Morgan, Edmund S. "The Puritans and Sex," *New England Quarterly* (Dec. 1942), XV, 591-607.

Morgan, Edmund S. *The Puritan Dilemma*. Boston: Little Brown, 1958.

____. *The Puritan Family: Religion and Domestic Relations in Seventeenth-Century New England*. New York: Harper & Row, 1944.

___. *Roger Williams: The Church and the State*. New York: W.W. Norton & Company, 1967.

___. Visible Saints: *The History of a Puritan Idea* (Ithaca: Cornell University Press, 1963).

Murphy, Andrew R. *Prodigal Nation: Moral Decline and Divine Punishment from New England to 9/11*. New York: Oxford University Press, 2009.

Noll, Mark A. *America's God: From Jonathan Edwards to Abraham Lincoln*. New York: Oxford University Press, 2002.

___.*In the Beginning Was the Word: The Bible in American Public Life, 1492-1783*. New York: Oxford University Press, 2016.

Noll, Mark A., George M. Rawlyk, and David W. Bebbington, eds., *Evangelicalism: Comparative Studies of Popular Protestantism of North America and the British Isles, 1700-1990*. New York: Oxford University Press, 1994.

Nuttall, Geoffrey. T*he Holy Spirit in Puritan Faith and Experience*. Oxford: Blackwell, 1946.

___. *Visible Saints: The Congregational Way, 1640-1660*. Oxford: Blackwell, 1957.

Orsi, Robert A. *History and Presence*. Cambridge: Harvard University Press, 2016.

Osterweis, Rollin G. *Three Centuries of New Haven, 1638-1938*. New Haven: Yale University Press, 1953.

Parker, Edwin Pond. *History of the Second Church of Christ in Hartford*. Hartford: Belknap and Warfield, 1892.

Pederson, Randall J. *Unity in Diversity: English Puritans and the Puritan Reformation, 1603-1689*. Leiden: Brill, 2014.

Perry, Charles Edward, ed. *Founders and Leaders of Connecticut, 1633-1783*. Boston: D.C. Heath, 1934.

Pestana, Carla. *The English Atlantic in an Age of Revolution, 1640-1661*. Cambridge: Harvard University Press, 2004.

___. *Liberty of Conscience and the Growth of Religious Diversity in Early America, 1636-1786*. Providence: John Carter Brown Library, 1986.

___. *Quakers and Baptists in Colonial Massachusetts*. New York: Cambridge University Press, 1991.

___. *Protestant Empire: Religion and the Making of the British Atlantic World*. Philadelphia: University of Pennsylvania Press, 2009.

___. "Religion" In *The British Atlantic World, 1500-1800*, edited by David Armitage and Michael J. Braddick, 69-89. New York: Palgrave Macmillan, 2002.

Peterson, Mark A. *The Price of Redemption: The Spiritual Economy of Puritan New England*. Palo Alto: Stanford University Press, 1997.

Peterson, Mark A. "Puritanism and Refinement in Early New England: Reflections on Communion Silver," *William and Mary Quarterly*, LVIII (2001), 307–346.

Pettit, Norman. *The Heart Prepared: Grace and Conversion in Puritan Spiritual Life*. New Haven: Wesleyan University Press, 1966.

Pope, Robert G. *The Half-Way Covenant: Church Membership in Puri-

tan New England. Princeton: Princeton University Press, 1969.

Powell, Sumner Chilton. *Puritan Village: The Formation of a New England Town*. Hanover: Wesleyan University Press, 1963.

Promey, Sally M. *Sensational Religion: Sensory Cultures in Material Practice*. New Haven: Yale University Press, 2014.

Rivett, Sarah. *The Science of the Soul in Colonial New England.* Chapel Hill: University of North Carolina Press, 2011.

Roth, David M. *Connecticut: A Bicentennial History.* New York: Norton, 1979.

Rust, Val D. *Radical Origins: Early Mormon Converts and Their Colonial Ancestors*. Chicago: University of Chicago Press, 2004.

Sanford, Elias B. *A History of Connecticut*. Hartford: S.S. Scranton, 1888.

Seeman, Erik R. "Lay Conversion Narratives: Investigating Ministerial Intervention," *New England Quarterly,* LXXI (1998), 629–634.

Seymour, Origen Storrs. *The Beginnings of the Episcopal Church in Connecticut. Connecticut Tercentenary Commission Publications, Number 30*. New Haven, Connecticut: Yale University Press, 1934.

Shipps, Jan. Mormonism: *The Story of a New Religious Tradition*. Urbana: University of Illinois Press, 1985.

Smith, Daniel Scott and J. David Hacker, "Cultural Demography: New England Deaths and the Puritan Perception of Risk," *Journal of Interdisciplinary History*, XXVI (1996), 380–383.

Smith, Daniel Scott and Michael S. Hindus, "Premarital Pregnancy in America, 1640–1971: An Overview and Interpretation," *Journal of Interdisciplinary History*, V (1975), 537–570.

Stannard, David E. *The Puritan Way of Death: A Study in Religion, Culture, and Social Change.* New York: Oxford University Press, 1977.

Stark, Rodney and William Sims Bainbridge. *A Theory of Religion.* New Brunswick: Rutgers University Press, 1996.

Stark, Rodney and William Sims Bainbridge. "Networks of Faith: Interpersonal Bonds and Recruitment to Cults and Sects," *American Journal of Sociology* 85 (1980): 1376-95.

Stark, Rodney and Roger Finke. *Acts of Faith: Explaining the Human Side of Religion.* Berkeley: University of California Press, 2000.

Starkey, Marion L. *The Congregational Way: The Role of the Pilgrims and Their Heirs in Shaping America.* Garden City: Doubleday, 1966.

Stout, Harry S. *The New England Soul: Preaching and Religious Culture in Colonial New England.* New York: Oxford University Press, 1986.

___. "Theological Commitment and American Religious History," *Theological Education*, 25 (1989), 44-59.

Stout, Harry S. and Robert M. Taylor, Jr. "Studies of Religion in American Society: The State of the Art," *New Directions in American Religious History*, edited by Harry S. Stout and D.G. Hart. New York: Oxford University Press, 1997.

Sullivan, Winnifred Fallers. *The Impossibility of Religious Freedom.* Princeton: Princeton University Press, 2005.

Sweet, William Warren. "The American Colonial Environment and Religious Liberty," *Church History*, (no. 4, 1935): 52.

Taylor, Robert J. *Colonial Connecticut: A History.* New York: KTO Press, 1979.

Tipson, Baird. "Invisible Saints: The 'Judgment of Charity' in the Early New England Churches," *Church History*, XLIV (1975), 460.

___."Samuel Stone's 'Discourse' against Requiring Church Relations," *William and Mary Quarterly*, XLVI (1989), 786–799.

Trumbull, Benjamin. *A Complete History of Connecticut, Civil and Ecclesiastical, From the Emigration of its First Planters, from England, in the Year 1630, to the Year 1764; and to the Close of the Indian Wars.* New London: H.D. Utley, 1898.

Ulrich, Laurel Thatcher. *Good Wives: Image and Reality in the Lives of Women in Northern New England, 1650-1750.* New York: Vintage, 1991.

___. "Virtuous Women Found: New England Ministerial Literature, 1668–1735," *American Quarterly*, XXVIII (1976), 22–23.

Valeri, Mark. Heavenly *Merchandize: How Religion Shaped Commerce in Puritan America*. Princeton: Princeton University Press, 2010.

Walker, Williston. *The Creeds and Platforms of Congregationalism.* New York: American Theological Library Association, 1893.

Waters, John. "Family, Inheritance, and Migration in Colonial New England: The Evidence from Guilford, Connecticut," *William and Mary Quarterly*, XXXIX (1982), 64–86.

Wilson, Lisa. Y*e Heart of a Man: The Domestic Life of Men in Colonial New England.* New Haven: Yale University Press, 1999.

Winiarski, Douglas L. *Darkness Falls on the Land of Light: Experiencing Religious Awakenings in Eighteenth-Century New England.* Chapel Hill: University of North Carolina Press, 2017.

___. "Gendered 'Relations' in Haverhill, Massachusetts, 1719–1742," in Peter Benes, ed., *In Our Own Words: New England Diaries, 1600 to the Present, I, Diary Diversity, Coming of Age, Annual Proceedings 2006–2007* (Boston: Dublin Seminar for New England Folklife, 2009), 66–67.

___. "Religious Experiences in New England," in Amanda Porterfield, ed., *Modern Christianity to 1900, A People's History of Christianity,* VI (Minneapolis: Fortress Press, 2007), 209–232.

Winship, Michael P. "Congregational Hegemony in New England, from the 1680s to the 1730s," in Stephen J. Stein, ed., *The Cambridge History of Religions in America, I, Pre-Columbian Times to 1790* (Cambridge: Cambridge University Press, 2012), 282–302.

___. *Making Heretics: Militant Protestantism and Free Grace in Massachusetts, 1636–1641.* Princeton: Princeton University Press, 2002.

___. *Seers of God: Puritan Providentialism in the Restoration and Early Enlightenment, Early America: History, Context, Culture* Baltimore: Johns Hopkins University, 1996.

Wuthnow, Robert. T*he Restructuring of American Religion.* Princeton: Princeton University Press, 1988.

Youngs, Jr., William T. "Congregational Clericalism: New England Ordinations Before the Great Awakening," *William and Mary*

Quarterly, XXXI (1974), 481–490.

Zimmerman, Philip D. "The Lord's Supper in Early New England: The Setting and the Service," in Peter Benes, ed., *New England Meeting House and Church: 1630–1850, Dublin Seminar for New England Folklife, Annual Proceedings* 1979 (Boston: Boston University1979), 130–133.

Zuckerman, Michael. *Peaceable Kingdoms: New England Towns in the Eighteenth Century*. New York: W. W. Norton & Company, 1970.

SOLA SCRIPTURA

Index

A

A Mid-Night Cry from the Temple of God
  communion, 46
  declension, 127
  divorce, 100
  faith, 59, 71, 125
  heresy, 59, 74
  marriage, 98, 100, 127
  salvation, 56 - 62 passim
Adams, Rev. Eliphalet, 32
  sympathizes with John Rogers, 85
Adultery, 58, 100, 101
African Americans, xvi, 6, 10, 14, 48, 111
  owned by James Rogers, 10
Ahlstrom, Sydney
  on Anne Hutchinson, 126
  on Rogerenes and Puritans, 126
American Protestantism
  challenged in early America, 123 - 134 passim
American Revolution, 54
  Rogerene influence on, 110
An Answer to a Book Lately Put Forth by Peter Pratt, 5n, 91n, 92n, 93n, 95, 101n
  on John Roger's divorce, 101
*An Impartial Relation of an Open and Publick Dispute Agreed upon Between Gurdon Saltonstal*l, 43 - 44
Anabaptism, xii, 8, 125n
Anglicanism, 2, 15, 16, 49, 50, 51, 53, 55, 104, 120
  and Rogerenes, 51
  Rogerenes's acceptance of, 51
Anglicans, 2, 2n, 55, 106, 122
Antinomian Crisis, 112
Appleby, Joyce, ix
Arabella (ship), xii, 126
Armageddon, 79
Arminianism, 113

B

Baptism, 91, 114
  John Rogers view of, 6, 8, 25n, 45, 47, 55, 60
Baptists, xii, 6, 8, 15, 16, 54, 55, 61n, 66, 75, 104, 105, 113, 125n, 131
Backus, Isaac
  coins term "Rogerenes," 15
Beckwith, Griswold
  marries Eliakim Cooley, Jr., 97
Beckwith, Matthew Jr.
  marries Elizabeth Griswold, 97

Beebe, Elizabeth (James Rogers, Sr.'s daughter)
  contests James Rogers's estate, 9 - 10
  marries Samuel Beebe, Jr. 118
Beebe, (Beeby), Samuel Sr., 118
Beebe, Samuel Jr., 19n
  fined for protesting ministerial tax, 76
  marries Elizabeth Rogers, 118
Bell Lane Sabbatarian Church (England)
  model for Newport Sabbatarians, 5, 21n, 61
Bible
  importance of John Rogers, xii, xvi, xii, 11, 17, 21, 26, 28, 29, 31,32, 35, 36, 40, 43, 45, 69, 70, 79, 84, 107, 120,122, 124 128
Black Lives Matter, xvi. See also, African Americans
Blinman, Rev. Richard, 3, 9
Block Island, RI, 103
Bolles, John, xiv, 66, 82, 109, 119
Bolles, John Jr.
  equal rights advocate, 113
  Rogerene, 111 - 113 passim
Bolles, Thomas, 13
Bonomi, Patricia,
  on Puritian divertsity, 131
Boston, MA, 1, 107, 110
Bradstreet, Rev. Simon, 3, 8, 116
Brekus, Catherine A.
  historiography of religion, 123, 123n, 130
Brewster, Rev. Nathaniel, 11
Briton, Ellen
  on Rogerene dissent, xv, 4n, 110
Brookhaven, L.I., 11
Buckley, Rev. Gershom., 3, 10, 11, 102
Burdick, Naomi
  marries Jonathan Rogers, 6
Byles, Rev. Mather Jr.
  persecutes Rogerenes, 110
  resigns as minister, 110

C

Calvinist ideals, 4, 5, 8, 56, 62, 121
Cambridge Association, 114
Canon-countercanon juxtaposition
  reveals colonial complexities, 123
Catholics, 104, 123n
Caulkins, Francis
  on John Rogers, 116, 128
Christ, 15, 16, 20, 23, 24, 25, 26, 27, 30, 34, 35, 42, 55, 56, 59, 65, 67, 69, 67, 70, 78, 80, 88, 89, 99, 106, 115, 121

Christopher, Richard, 32
Christophers, John, 117
Chu, Jonathan
　on Quaker dissenters, 61, 116
Cohn, Henry S.
　on colonial divorce, 101
Coles, Sarah
　marries John Rogers, 103
　personality, 103
Communal worship, 21, 35, 37, 43
　John Rogers advocates, 21
Communion, 14, 46, 47, 63, 113
Congregational Book of Confession, 33
Congregational Church of New London (CT), 3, 4, 6, 8, 10, 34, 43, 44, 48, 92, 110, 114, 118
　James Rogers joins, 10
Congregational Confession of Faith, 77
Congregational law, 62, 76, 85, 91, 96, 102, 117
Congregationalism, 37, 59, 61, 62, 66, 75, 76, 92, 105, 106, 119
　significance of meetinghouse to, 3, 10, 14, 23, 33, 34, 36, 39, 40, 45, 50, 65, 73, 74, 76n, 78, 82, 84, 91, 104, 110, 112
　women, 19, 25, 60, 62, 71, 77, 91, 100, 101, 103 - 105, 110, 112
Congregationalists, vi, xi 2, 3, 56, 57. 64, 67, 69, 70, 71, 72, 75 - 84 passim, 86, 87, 88, 89, 91, 105, 107, 113 - 118 passim
　and Anglicans, 2, 2n, 55, 106, 122
　and John Rogers, xiii, 15, 16, 19, 20, 23, 25, 27, 28, 31, 32 - 44 passim, 46 - 50 passim,
　as religious dissenters, 122
　baptism, 8, 46, 48, 52, 62, 113
　First-Day Sabbath, 14, 21, 22, 23, 25, 26, 27, 28, 30, 31, 32, 33, 35, 36, 37, 38
Connecticut
　Congregationalist morals in, 35
　liberal divorce laws, 103
　view of unmarried mothers, 103
Cooley, Eliakim Jr.
　marries Griswold Beckwoth, 97
Court of Assistants (Hartford)
　and Rogerenes, 49, 76
Crandall, John
　baptizes John Rogers into Sabbatarianism, 6
Culver, Edward, 13
Culver, John, 13, 121

D

DACA (Deferred Action for Childhood Arrivals), xvi
Danforth, Rev. Samuel
　decline of Puritan mission, 126 - 127

Denominationalism, 114
Dialectica
　and John Rogers, 124
Dissenters, ix, xii, xiii, 2, 2n, 5, 7, 28, 29, 34, 48 - 51 passim, 60, 66, 68, 105, 125 - 126, 129
　Anglicans as, 52
　Congregationalists as, 97, 120
　historians' quandry, 125 - 126
　Quakers as, 120
　Rogerenes as, 55, 68, 113, 116
　women, 104 - 105, 112
　Congregationalists persecution of, 59, 116, 120, 129
Divorce, 98, 100, 101,105
　Anna Griswold encourages daughter, 91 - 92
　Elizabeth Griswold Rogers, xiii, xvii, 92 - 93, 97, 99 - 100
　John Rogers, 91, 93, 96, 99, 100
　John, Jr. on, 91, 101

E

Edmundson, William, 7, 60
Ely, Justice William, 44
England, xii, 2, 5, 15, 16, 21n, 48, 49, 51, 60, 61, 76 - 77, 87, 101, 126

F

First Congregational Church of Milford (CT), 4
First Congregational Church of New London (CT), 3, 4, 6, 8, 10, 34, 43, 44, 48, 92, 110, 114, 118
First-Day Sabbath, 14, 21, 22, 23, 25, 26, 27, 28, 30, 31, 32, 33, 35, 36, 37, 38. See also, Sabbath.
Fitch, James Rev.,
　critical of John Rogers, 36 - 37
　on First-Day Sabbath, 36 - 37
Fog Plain (New London), 13
Fornication, 100, 103
Fox, Mrs. Bathshua R.(Rogers daughter)
　as dissenter, 10, 86
　marriage to Samuel Fox, 104, 118
Fox, George, 57
Fox, Samuel, 104, 118
　marriage to Bathsheba Smith, 104, 118

G

General Court of Connecticut
　upholds Congregational theocracy, 49
Gortonists, vii
Goshen, CT
　Rogers land in, 13
Great Awakening, 110
Green, Timothy, 30 - 31
Griswold, Anna 11, 91 - 92

158

on John Rogers, 91
Griswold, Elizabeth
   divorce from John Rogers, 91 - 94, 101
   dowry, 11
   infatuation of John Rogers, 79
   John Rogers, Jr. on, 91, 101
   marriage to Matthew Beckwith, Jr., 97
   marriage to John Rogers, 4n, 5, 11, 91
   marriage to Peter Pratt, Sr., 94
   returns to Congregationalism, 74
   See also Elizabeth Griswold Rogers
Griswold, Matthew, 11, 91, 92, 92n, 93, 99
Grosskopf, Denise
   on Rogerenes, xiin

H
Half-Way Covenant, xii, 162
Hall, David D., 75, 131
   role of printers, 75
Hartford, CT, 60, 76, 82, 93, 113
Hill, Mercy
   wins custody of children, 93
Hiscox, Thomas, 8
"Hiving-off", 39
Horton, Joseph
   fined for not keeping Sunday Sabbath, 7
Hough, William, 10
Hubbard, Samuel, 8
Hutchinson, Anne, vii, 29, 112, 125n, 126
   Perry Miller on, 112, 125 - 126
   use of Scripture, 29
Hutchinsonians, xi

I
Idolatry, 23, 28
Individualism
   American principle of, 50 - 52, 122
   and John Rogers, 21, 35, 38 - 42 passim, 45, 52, 63, 69, 88, 89, 106, 110, 111, 121, 122, 125
   Congregationalists distrust, 36, 125
   reduces church authority, 45
Israel, 24, 25, 30, 98, 99, 124, 125

J
Jackson, John, 48
   African American follower of Rogerene faith, 14
Japhet
   Native American servant, 14, 74n
Jews and Jewish tradition, 21, 125n
Jesus, See Christ
Jones, Robert
   marries Mary Ransford, 103

L
Land
   abundance of counter to Congregational precepts, 39
   significance of, 39
"Land of Steady Habits," 4, 35. See also Connecticut.
Latham, Cary, 10 - 11
Liveen, John, 8
Long Island, NY, 11, 48, 60,87, 103
Luther, Martin, 58, 74, 76
Lyme, CT, 94, 97
Lynde, Justice Nathaniel, 44

M
Mamacock Farm, 92, 107, 109
Marriage, 101, 103
Marty, Martin
   on American religious canon, 123
Massachusetts, 56
Mather, Rev. Cotton, 113, 125, 126
Mather, Increase, 113
Mather, Richard, 1113
McLoughlin, William G.
   on Baptists, 131
   on Rogerenes, 75
Mead, Sidney
   land in colonial Connecticut, 39
Meetinghouses, 3, 10, 19, 23, 33, 34, 38, 39, 40, 45, 50, 65, 73, 74n, 76, 82, 84, 91, 104, 110, 112
Middlekauff, Robert, ix, 125
Miller, Perry
   on Anne Hutchinson, 112, 125 - 126
   Congregationalism, 113, 128, 130
   Roger Williams, 108
Montville, CT, 118
Morals
   Congregationalist view, 35
Moses, 25, 29, 67, 83, 98
Mumford, Stephen, 21
Mystic, CT, 13, 81

N
Narragansetts, 11
Native Americans, 10, 11, 12, 14, 110, 111, 112, 118
New England
   diversity of, 111
New England,
   acceptance of John Rogers, 120, 121, 133, 134
   communal nature, 100
   dissenters, xii, 1, 2n, 28, 49, 54, 59, 60, 61, 66, 77, 114, 116
   idealism in, 113, 114

159

marriage and divorce in, 101, 103, 105
piety of, 124 - 125, 127
population of, 128
Puritans in, x, 16, 53, 66, 127, 128
Rogerenes in, 120, 121, 133, 134
Sabbath in, 22, 23, 36, - 40 passim
New Haven, CT, 2, 113
New London, CT, vii, viii, 10, 40, 55,
   and Rogerenes, 14, 16, 17, 19, 34, 54, 55, 57, 59, 73, 74, 75, 76, 79, 115, 117, 118, 119
   as heterogeneous port city, 1, 13, 113, 119
   Congregationalits in, 3, 4, 8
      and Rogerenes, 83, 114, 115, 117 - 119 passim
   dissenters in, xi, xii, xvii, 1, 2, 2n, 3, 7, 8, 9, 19, 37, 60, 61, 117, 119,
   Gurdon Saltonstall and, 43 - 44
   James Rogers in, 116, 121
   John Rogers and, xiii, 7, 19, 33, 34, 73, 74, 81, 82, 84, 85, 102 - 103, 116, 120, 121
   Mary Ransford Rogers in, 96, 102 - 104
   population, 2
   printshops, 75
   Rogerenes in, 14, 16, 17, 19, 34, 73 - 76 passim, 79, 115, 117 - 119 passim
   Sabbath in, 20, 22, 23, 32, 37 - 38
Newport Sabbatarian Church, 5
95 Theses, 58
Norwich Congregational Church, 36 - 37
Norwich, CT, 37
Noyes, James, xii

O

Orthodox and dissenter
   terms explained, 126
Orthodoxy, xi,36, 45, 46, 61, 92, 113, 120, 123, 124, 129, 130, 130n, 132
Owaneco (Native American), 119

P

Papists, 15. 16
Pequots, 11
Pestana, Carla
   on American religious history, 112
Pharisees
   John Rogers on, 6, 23, 41, 66
Piety, 8, 112, 113, 114, 119, 124, 129
Planned Parenthood, xvi
Pratt, Peter
   marries Elizabeth Griswold, 94
Pratt, Peter Jr.
   embraces Rogerene doctrine, 94
   on John Rogers, 95
   renounces Rogerene doctrine, 94 - 95

Predestination, 5, 55, 56 - 57, 121,
Prentis, Stephen
   marries John Rogers's daughter, Elizabeth, 95
Presbyterians, 3, 15, 76n
Printers, 73, 74, 75, 87
Protestant dissenters
   Congregationalists regarded as, 48 - 49
Puritan dilemma, 125 - 126
Puritanism, 120
Puritans, xi, xii, xiii, 16, 53, 66, 106n, 111, 112, 123, 124, 125, 125n, 126, 128, 130, 132

Q

Quakers, xii, 2n, 16, 54, 55, 57, 58, 60, 61, 66, 75, 104, 105, 106, 113, 115, 116, 120
"Quaker laws", 50

R

Ramist logic, 124
Ransford, Mary, 96, 102 - 104 passim
   alledged cross-dresser, 96
   and John Rogers, 98, 99, 102, 103
   as Rogerene, 104
   assault charges, 96
   children out of wedlock, 102, 103
   contentious personality, 96, 104
   leaves New London and abandons children, 104
   marries Robert Jones, 103
   relationship with John, Jr, 96, 97.
   separation from John Rogers, 103
Religion, x, 1-17 passim, 19, 39, 47, 49, 52, 54, 56, 62, 63, 70, 77, 114, 118, 123, 123n, 130
Remington, Mary. See Mary Ransford
Rhode Island, 1, 2n, 39, 74, 103, 125n
Robinson, William, religious martyr, 115
Rogerenes
   afterlife, 80
   as dissenters, 53, 58, 69, 87, 90
   background, xvi, 4, 5, 6, 8 - 15 passim, 19n
   church vs. state, 81
   communion and, 46
   Congregationalists, xiv,16, 19, 22, 23, 25, 33, 34, 35, 36, 43, 46, 50, 55, 59, 60, 73, 75, 76n, 78, 81, 88, 89, 101, 112, 116, 117, 118, 119
   Bible's importance to, 70, 120
   civil acceptance, 116 - 119 passim
   communal worship, 21, 22, 37, 40, 44
   Congregationalist relations, ix, 15, 23, 31, 34, 35, 48, 55, 63, 66, 70, 81, 90 92, 97
   doctrine, xii, 8, 38, 59, 86, 87, 91, 97, 99, 100, 105
   equal rights advocates, 111

flaying membership, 116
forms of dissent, 55
growth of sect, 14
impact on American consciousness, 110, 122
in New London, 120, 121, 133, 34
individualism and, 45
intellectual enlightment and, 70, 71
labeled fringe sect, 17, 34,
leverage wealth to advance beliefs, 99
marriage and divorce, 101, 103
marginalized, 52, 133
Native Americans and, 11, 12, 111
persecution of, 33, 34, 51, 79, 80, 82 - 88 passim, 110
predestination, 55, 121
radicalism, 120
religious pagentry, 67
role of women, 104 - 105
Sabbath, xiv, xvi, 5, 6, 7, 8, 14, 19 - 34 passim, 35, 36, 37, 38, 43, 45, 46, 49, 50, 55, 70, 78, 82, 83, 85, 87, 104, 110, 117, 120, 121, 123
slavery, 55, 111
spiritualism, 63, 64
suspected of burning meetinghouse, 82
Sydney Ahlstrom on, 126
test societal limits, 99
thoughts on communion, 47
views on sacraments, 82
use of courts, 49, 50, 76 - 77
use of print, xiii, xvi, 73, 74, 75, 76, 109
William McLoughlin on, 57
Rogers, Bathsheba, 4, 4n, 10, 82, 83, 109, 118
Rogers, Elizabeth (daughter of John and Elizabeth Griswold Rogers) 4, 5
baptism, 8
marries Stephen Prentis, 94
Rogers, Elizabeth Griswold, xvii, 4n, 8, 13, 91, 92n, 93, 94, 99, 107, 118
as Sabbatarian, 91 - 92
denounces Sabbatarianism, 92
divorces John Rogers, xiii, 92 - 93
first woman in America to win custody of children, 93
marries John Rogers, 4n, 5, 91
religious transformation, 91 - 93
Rogers, Gershom
bastard son of John Rogers, 102
Rogers, James, Sr., xvi, 4, 4n, 9, 10, 11, 12, 13, 14, 116
Rogers, James Jr.,10, 19n, 50, 76, 83
Rogers, John, vii
accused of polygamy and hypocrisy, 97, 98
allegations against, 6

Congregationalism, 37, 39, 59,61, 62, 66, 77, 78, 105, 106, 119
Gurdon Saltonstall, 43 - 44, 85, 110, 117, 125
and James Rogers's estate, 10
and meetinghouses, 3, 10, 19, 23, 33, 34, 38, 39, 40, 45, 50, 65, 73, 74n, 76, 82, 84, 91, 104,110, 112
and Rev. James Fitch, 36
and Scripture, xi, xii, xiii, xvi, xvii, 7, 8, 15, 16, 17, 19, 20, 21, 25, 26, 28 - 34 passim, 36, 37, 38, 43 - 47 passim, 50, 51, 54, 55, 59, 65, 67 - 72 passim, 77, 78, 89, 91, 93, 98, 99, 100, 102, 106, 109, 111, 114, 120, 121, 121n
arrest, 117
as dissenter, 53, 55
assualt charges, 86
Augustinian influence, 111, 124
background, 4
baptizes sister-in-law, 8
becomes pastor of New London Seventh Day Baptist Church, 7
beliefs about the Sabbath, xiv, xvi, 5, 6, 7, 8, 14, 19 - 34 passim, 35, 36, 37, 38, 43, 45, 46, 49, 50, 55, 70, 78, 82, 83, 85, 87, 104, 110, 117, 120, 121,123
beastiality charges, 93
businessman, 119
charged for fathering children out of wedlock, 100, 102
charged with felony for escaping goal, 86
civic role in New London, 96
conversion experience, 6
courts, 49, 50, 76 - 77
death from smallpox, 107
defines fornication versus adultery, 100, 103
domestic violence, 79
Elizabeth Griswold, xiii, 4, 5, 13, 58, 73, 74, 75, 76, 78, 79, 81, 88
estate, 107
father purchases farm for, 9
fined for not observing Sunday Sabbath, 33, 42, 58, 65
gains townspeople's sympathies, 85, 117
generosity of, 106
Gurdon Saltonstall, 43, 44 - 45, 85, 110
heterodox views, 92, 93
impact on New London, 106
imprisoned, 82- 83, 85 - 87, 89, 117
individualism, 21, 35, 38 - 42 passim, 45, 52, 63, 69, 88, 89, 106, 110, 111, 121, 122, 125
interactions with Europe shaped theology of, 119
leadership, 62 - 67 passim

161

loses custody of children, 93
madness accusations, 86, 87, 91
marriages, 4n, 5, 11, 91, 102, 103, 105
Congregationalist relationships, ix, 15, 23, 31, 34, 35, 48, 55, 63, 66, 70, 81, 90 92, 97
doctrine, xii, 8, 38, 59, 86, 87,89, 91, 97, 99, 100, 105
on divorce, 92 - 93, 100, 101, 103, 105, 106
on marriage, 98 - 105, passim, 127
on polygamy, 97, 98
Sola Scriptura, 28
New Covenant, 25
opposes taxes, 5, 40, 49, 66
pacifist doctrine, 89
Quakers, 115, 116
questions Sabbatarian doctrines, 7
refutes Rev. Benjamin Wadsworth, 22, 28, 29, 30, 32
143
relationship with offspring, 94, 95
religious beliefs, xiii, 25, 39, 38, 40, 43, 44, 47, 51, 87, 93
reputation, 19, 116 - 119
refutes First-Day Sabbath, 14, 28, 31, 37
secularization in New London, 113 -114
separation from Mary Ransford, 103, 104
separation of church and state, 53
theologian, 29, 55
use of courts, 49, 50, 76 - 77
whipped, 19, 33, 83, 120
"wig" episode, 43, 44, 67
women's rights, 105
Rogers, John, Jr., 17, 48
arrested, 83
birth, 5
critical of grandmother, 91, 92n
death,110
father's imprisonment, 85 - 86, 117
influence on Peter Pratt, Jr., 94
on parents' divorce, 101
persecution of, 85 - 86, 117
reputation, 109
turbulent relationship with Mary Ransford, 50, 96
Rogers, John III, 66, 109
Rogers, John IV, 110, 111
importance of conscience, 111
Rogers, Jonathan,
as Rogerene, 12, 76
marries Naomi Burdick, 6
refutes Rogerene practices, xiv
Rogers, Joseph, 4
father purchases farm for, 10
fined for not keeping Sunday Sabbath, 7

Rogers, Mary
bastard daughter of John Rogers, 102
Rogers, Ransford, 104
Rogers, Samuel, 12, 84, 118
Rogers, Sarah
James Rogers, Jr. sues, 50
Rowland, Elizabeth
divorces John Rogers, 4n, 96

S
Sabbatarianism, 6,7, 8 , 9, 92, 119
Sabbatarians, xii, 5, 6, 8, 21, 21n, 22n, 54, 55, 59, 60, 61, 66, 68, 70, 75, 88, 91, 106, 113, 120
Sabbath, xiv, xvi, 5, 6, 7, 8, 12, 19 - 34 passim, 35, 36, 37, 38, 43, 45, 46, 49, 50, 70, 78, 85, 110, 120
See also First-Day Sabbath
Rogerenes and, xiv, xvi, 5, 6, 7, 8, 14, 19 - 34 passim, 35, 36, 37, 38, 43, 45, 46, 49, 50, 55, 70, 8, 82, 83, 85, 87, 104, 110, 117, 120, 121, 123
Saltonstall, Gov. Gurdon, xiii, 3, 4
and John Rogers, 44, 85, 87, 110
wig episode", 43, 44, 67
Saybrook Platform, 3
Saybrook, CT, 10
Scripture, xi, - xvii, 7, 8, 15, 16, 17, 21, 25, 26, 28 - 34 passim, 36, 37, 38, 43 - 47 passim, 50, 51, 54, 55, 59, 65, 67 - 72 passim, 77, 78, 89, 91, 93, 98, 99, 100, 102,106, 109, 111, 114, 120, 121, 121n, 124, 125, 126, 129
Sectarianism and Sectarians, xi, xii, xiii, xvi, 1, 2, 3, 7, 8, 12, 14 - 17 passim, 28, 34, 38, 40, 46, 47, 50, 51, 53, 55, 60 - 63 passim, 66, 68, 75, 79, 81, 86, 103, 105, 106, 111, 114 - 120 passim, 123 - 126 passim, 128 - 130, passim, 132
Secularization, 93
Seventh Day Baptist Church (New London), 7, 21n
Seventh-Day Sabbath, 25, 29, 30
Seventh-Day Baptists, viii, 6, 7
Shepard, Thomas
on Congregational Sabbath, 20
Short, Thomas
New London printer, 75
Sins, 6, 20, 24, 28, 56, 58, 59, 61, 80, 127
Smallpox, 107, 109
John Rogers contracts, 107
Smith, Bathsheba Rogers, 4, 10, 82, 109, 118
Smith, Bathshua (James Rogers' s daughter), 10, 76
Smith, Bethsheba
Rogerene, 98
Smith, John, 10

Smith, Richard
  fined for not keeping Sunday Sabbath, 7
Society for the Propagation of the Gospel in Foreign Parts, 2
Sola Scriptura, vii, 101
  John Rogers belief in, 28
Standing Order, xiii, 32, 34, 43, 75, 105, 106, 111, 117
Steer(e), Richard
  fined as Rogerene, 49, 76
  petitions court for religious liberty, 51
Stevenson, Marmaduke, religious martyr, 105
Stoddard, Solomon, 114
Stubens (Stebbins), John, 12, 13
Stubbins, Daniel, 92
Sunday Sabbath, 7, 20, 21, 23, 117

T
Ten Commandments, 5
  and John Rogers, 21, 29, 124
Tender years doctrine, 93
The Book of the Revelation of Jesus Christ and John Rogers a Servant of Jesus Christ, 106
The Day of Doom, 128
The New England Mind: The Seventeenth Century
  importance of, 112
The Prey Taken From the Strong
  anti-Rogerene tract, 95
Toleration Act of 1708, 50, 51
Toleration Acts of 1689, 50, 51
Tongue, Elizabeth, 1
Tubs, Mary, 92

U
Uncas (Native American), 120

V
Visible Saints, 10, 124

W
Wadsworth, Rev. Benjamin, 22, 28, 29, 30
  and John Rogers, 29, 30, 32
Waterhouse, Jacob
  Rogerene, 12, 13
Waterhouse, John
  Rogerene, 109
Wells, ME, 13
Wetherell, Capt. Daniel, 44, 117
Wetherell, Judge, 102
Whipple, Samuel, 19, 33, 110, 111
"Wig" episode
  and John Rogers, 43, 44, 67
Wigglesworth, Michael
  Day of Doom, 128
Williams, Roger, xii, 28, 75, 125n 126
Winthrop, Gov. Fitz-John, 1, 102
Winthrop, John, viii, 106
  and visible saints, 124
Winthrop, John Jr., 1, 9
Winthrop's Cove (New London), 8
Winthrop, Wait Still, 1
Wittenberg, Germany, 76
Women, 19, 25, 60, 62, 71, 77, 91, 99, 100, 101, 103 - 105, 110, 112
  and Congregationalism, 86
  and sectarianism, 86
  as dissenters, 85
  John Rogers on, 87
Worth, William, 73

Y
Young, Thomas, 117

www.ingramcontent.com/pod-product-compliance
Lightning Source LLC
Chambersburg PA
CBHW070736020526
44118CB00035B/1400